BRAIN WAVES

VICTORIAN BRITAIN

John Corn

Contents

The Victorians	The Sun Never Sets …	6	*Housing*	Time Traveller	28
	The Victoria Line	7		Civic Pride	29
	Generation Game	8		Home Sweet Home	30
	Great Victorians	9		Parlour Games 1 & 2	31-32
	When I'm Sixty-four	10		Homework	33
Transport	Turnpikes	11	*Food*	Changing Places	34
	Canals	12		Open All Hours 1 & 2	35-36
	Iron Horses	13		What's Cooking?	37
	Going Loco	14		The Good Seed On The Land	38
	Takes Your Breath Away	15			
Work	Workshop Of The World	16	*Play*	Antiques Roadshow	39
	The Price Of Coal	17		Moving Pictures	40
	You Rang M'Lord 1 & 2	18-19		Away Day	41
	Street Directories	20		Didn't We Have A Lovely Time?	42
	Plough The Fields And Scatter	21		That's The Way To Do It!	43
Public Health and Religion	Where There's Muck	22	*Schools*	Shed Street School	44
	Fatal Diseases	23		Move With The Times	45
	In Loving Memory	24		Copy Book	46
	At Rest	25		Dear Diary	47
	Sunday	26		The End Of An Era	48
	Brave New World	27			

Folens Publishers

Introduction

Victorian Britain is one of the core study units outlined in the National Curriculum. All of the repro-masters and notes contained within this book cover the three attainment targets of:
Knowledge and understanding of history
Interpretations of history
The use of historical sources.
They are specific to levels 1-4.

There are eight sections within the book covering:
the reign of Queen Victoria
transport
work
public health
religion
housing
food and farming
leisure
education.

Although these are produced with an obvious historical bias, most involve other curriculum areas. The sheets are designed to be practical, visually stimulating and should be used to support existing materials and teacher input. They should not be worked through methodically but should be modified and amended as required in order to develop and extend certain aspects of historical enquiry.

Folens books are protected by international copyright laws. All rights reserved. The copyright of all materials in this book, except where otherwise stated, remains the property of the publisher and author. No part of this publication may be reproduced, stored in a retrieval system, or transmitted, in any form or by any means, for whatever purpose, without the written permission of Folens Limited.

Folens do allow photocopying of selected pages of this publication for educational use, providing that this use is within the confines of the purchasing institution. You may make as many copies as you require for classroom use of the pages so marked.

This resource may be used in a variety of ways; however, it is not intended that teachers or students should write into the book itself.

© 1993 Folens Limited, on behalf of the author.

First published 1993 by Folens Limited, Albert House, Apex Business Centre, Boscombe Road, Dunstable, LU5 4RL, England.

ISBN 185276342-6

Illustrations by: David Carpenter.
Cover: Hybert Design and Type.
Cover photograph: © Leeds City Council.
Other photographs: Hulton Picture Library.
Printed by Craft Print Pte Ltd, Singapore

Acknowledgements:
Mathew Gloag & Sons Ltd.
Mr Matt Burghardt.

Teachers' Notes

The Sun Never Sets ...
A good up to date political map of the world is needed, preferably of a projection similar to that used on the sheet. Chart information could be put on a data base.

The Victoria Line
The information on Queen Victoria's family tree could be re-drawn by the children as a mobile with the Queen's children drawn in and coloured on the reverse. Card should be used for this. The children's family tree can be shown through photographs and displayed. Use telephone directories, yellow pages and street plans to locate streets and buildings named 'Victoria'. A picture map can be made from the results.

Generation Game
Use a calculator for this game in order to hurry it along. The small pictures can be enlarged, coloured and used to form a time-line.

Great Victorians
A selection of library books and encyclopedias will be needed.

When I'm Sixty-four
A familiar looking game to introduce or reinforce some of the main events in Queen Victoria's reign. Counters should be coloured as a 'penny red' and a 'penny black' and are best mounted on card. A dice is needed.

Turnpikes
Map local turnpikes and investigate charges - the archive section of the local library should be able to help. An introduction to old-fashioned money and its modern equivalent is useful here. Investigating and 'making' roads like those devised by Telford and MacAdam makes a good display.

Canals
Again imperial measurements are used and they may need to be explained. The sheet can be used as part of a project on canals including: canal builders, networks, how locks work and life on the canal. The technological change between turnpikes, canals and later railways should be emphasised.

Iron Horses
An enlargement to A3 would increase the space available for drawing the pictures. As with canals, extensive work on 'railway mania' can be set in motion using the sheet as appropriate. The decline of the railways in the latter half of the twentieth century due to the motor car and Dr Beeching could be briefly mentioned.

Going Loco
A railway building game looking at the effects of topography on railway construction. Areas identified as low, high or mountainous should be shaded lightly in different colours first of all. Actual charges can be reduced to 1, 2 or 3 to replace the more difficult thousands and help calculations. Discuss railway features such as embankment, viaduct and cutting.

Takes Your Breath Away
Compare old advertisements with modern ones in such areas as price, performance and style of the vehicle as well as the style of the advertisement. A time line showing the development of the motor car is eye catching. Collect brochures from motor dealers.

Workshop Of The World
A comparison of the length of a Victorian working day with a modern school day is striking. Conduct a half hour lesson in line with the 1842 factory rules. Include a high reading and writing content. Ask the children how they feel afterwards. Drama is useful here.

The Price Of Coal
Every history textbook concerned with Victorian times examines working conditions, especially those of children. This sheet can be seen as an introduction. A time-line showing improvements in working conditions can be drawn and displayed along with a 'caption' type commentary. Again, drama is useful.

You Rang M'Lord 1 & 2
Conduct interviews for jobs in domestic service after writing a job description. Census material can be used to show how common work in domestic service was. Reminiscences are interesting to listen to but difficult to obtain unless recorded and kept by a local oral history unit or local archive section.

Street Directories
Transfer the ideas and information here to a local street directory extract. A picture map can be drawn. The children can draw and colour a picture of the occupation and link it to the correct house on a map. Use a 1:1250 scale map as these give the most detail and enlarge the study area as much as possible. Make a Venn diagram to show jobs found only in Victorian times, jobs done today and ones that have changed a little.

Plough The Fields And Scatter
Hidden words - weeding, turnips, hay, harvest, cows, potatoes, birds, stones, firewood and pigs.

Where There's Muck
This sheet can open up a whole area of work on public health and living conditions. For familiarity, concentrate on a local urban environment and collect evidence: photographs, maps, accounts and notices. Display them as a local projection on this theme. Compare the quality of life here to that of a wealthier Victorian suburb.

Fatal Diseases
There is a strong link with science here regarding the nature and spread of disease. Work on the growth of hospitals and medical developments can be tackled. Look at cures for these diseases then and now.

In Loving Memory
A genuine letter reproduced in its original form complete with 'errors'. A Victorian churchyard survey should follow. Record names, ages and occupations for making graphs. Collect wax crayon rubbings of decorations and dates. Record the type of memorial itself: chest, table, headstone, pedestal and rustic. Find the most common. A full list can be found in Brain Waves *Built Environment*. Compare the results with a modern graveyard. Data bases are useful.

At Rest
A classroom-based churchyard survey. Encourage speculation as to why some people should live longer than others.

© Folens Ltd.

Teachers' Notes

Sunday
A class discussion as to what makes a 'Sunday' should be undertaken focusing on activities that occur at the times given. 5cm² graph paper can be used for the picture frieze and a commentary attached underneath.

Brave New World
When each 'cartoon' is significantly enlarged (to A4 or even A3 size) with its caption, an impressive display can be made. Position them as a time-line. The date of each development is hidden within the cartoon.

Time Traveller
Encourage the children to write in the style of a reporter but to express a personal view about events - these can be compared and discussed. Children should be encouraged to distinguish between fact and point of view.

Civic Pride
The population of Great Britain increased from 10.5 million in 1801 to 37 million in 1901. The most significant increase took place in London and northern industrial towns. Further statistics:

1801			1901	
London	1 117 000			6 500 000
Bolton	18 000			168 000
Glasgow	77 000			905 000
Sheffield	46 000			380 000

The difference between fact and point of view should be discussed and children encouraged to provide examples based on the school or local environment. Collections can be made.

Home Sweet Home
A selection of local maps will be needed, scale 1:1250 is best, copies of which can usually be obtained very cheaply from the local planning office. If a standard of eight persons in each dwelling is used, a measure of population density can be estimated. Look at areas of Victorian housing. Notice a decline in density away from a city centre.

Parlour Games 1 & 2
For best results enlarge these sheets to A3 size or paste on to card. Children can work in pairs. These will make an excellent display. Enhance it with extracts from 'Laura Ashley' type wallpapers, borders and so on. Compare with a modern lounge displayed in the same way.

Homework
A selection of mail-order catalogues will be needed. Museum services will often supply Victorian domestic artefacts. Again compare them with modern ones.

Changing Places
The best development here is to undertake a village survey picking out Victorian detail such as footscrapers, stained glass, stables - a photo trail is useful. Look for change in the village both in the field and by studying old and modern maps. An aerial photograph could be used.

Open All Hours 1 & 2
Enlarge to A3 if possible. These should be displayed alongside enlarged Victorian advertisements.

What's Cooking?
Comparisons should be on ingredients and style of kitchen management.

The Good Seed On The Land
This can develop into a farm game. Weather lore can be collected and paintings made and displayed.

Antiques Roadshow
Antique toys borrowed from a museum service add interest.

Moving Pictures
Work in pairs. This can make an unusual and interesting display if an enlarged copy of the central flick book character is mounted and displayed next to the flick book.

Away Day
Some work on the Great Exhibition is needed.

Didn't We Have a Lovely Time?
Photocopy on to card if possible so that a postcard can be made. Discussion is essential prior to completion of the chart concerning the differences between Victorian and modern resorts. Display with modern postcards from British resorts.

That's The Way To Do It!
Introduce the characters and possible plots. Mount the finished booth on to a card base to make it more stable.

Shed Street School
The substance of each subject area needs to be described to the children as well as the type of discipline used. Go through the class timetable or daily routine as a comparison.

Move With The Times
Making a mobile. In many old schools evidence of Victorian times can still be found. Such evidence needs to be pointed out and recorded or photographed and perhaps made into a trail. The caretaker is often useful here.

Copy Book
Try to re-create the atmosphere of a Victorian classroom. Rank the desks and insist on complete silence. Introduce a cane - but do not use it! Insist that pupils use only their right hand, even left-handed pupils. Demonstrate copperplate on the blackboard. Again try to compare a Victorian classroom with a modern one.

Dear Diary
Pick out items in the school log book from times past and devise questions about them. A class log book could be made and filled in by different children, in copperplate of course.

The End Of An Era
A round-up of all work introduced in the book. Questions need to be carefully devised - a difficult task requiring close guidance and answers similarly rehearsed. Newspaper items, when written, will make an excellent display. Enlarge the bottom section of the sheet for maximum effect. Word processing is useful.

© Folens Ltd.

Brain Waves Victorian Britain – Key Elements	Chronology	Range and depth of Historical Knowledge and Understanding	Interpreting of History	Historical Enquiry	Organisation and Communication
The Sun Never Sets		✓			
The Victoria Line	✓			✓	
Generation Game	✓				
Great Victorians	✓	✓			✓
When I'm Sixty Four	✓	✓			
Turnpikes		✓			
Canals		✓	✓		
Iron Horses	✓	✓		✓	✓
Going Loco		✓		✓	
Takes Your Breath Away		✓			
Workshop of the World		✓	✓	✓	
The Price of Coal		✓		✓	✓
You Rang M'Lord 1		✓			
You Rang M'Lord 2		✓			
Street Directories		✓	✓	✓	✓
Plough the Fields and Scatter		✓			
Where There's Muck		✓	✓	✓	✓
Fatal Diseases		✓			
In Loving Memory				✓	✓
At Rest		✓	✓	✓	✓
Sunday		✓			
Brave New World	✓	✓		✓	
Time Traveller			✓	✓	
Civic Pride		✓			✓
Home Sweet Home		✓		✓	✓
Parlour Games 1		✓			
Parlour Games 2		✓		✓	
Homework		✓		✓	✓
Changing Places		✓			
Open All Hours 1			✓	✓	
Open All Hours 2		✓			
What's Cooking?		✓		✓	✓
The Good Seed on the Land		✓			
Antiques Roadshow				✓	
Moving Pictures		✓			
Away Day		✓		✓	
Didn't We Have a Lovely Time?		✓		✓	✓
That's the Way to Do It!		✓			
Shed Street School		✓			✓
Move With the Times		✓		✓	✓
Copy Book		✓			
Dear Diary		✓	✓	✓	✓
The End of an Era	✓			✓	✓

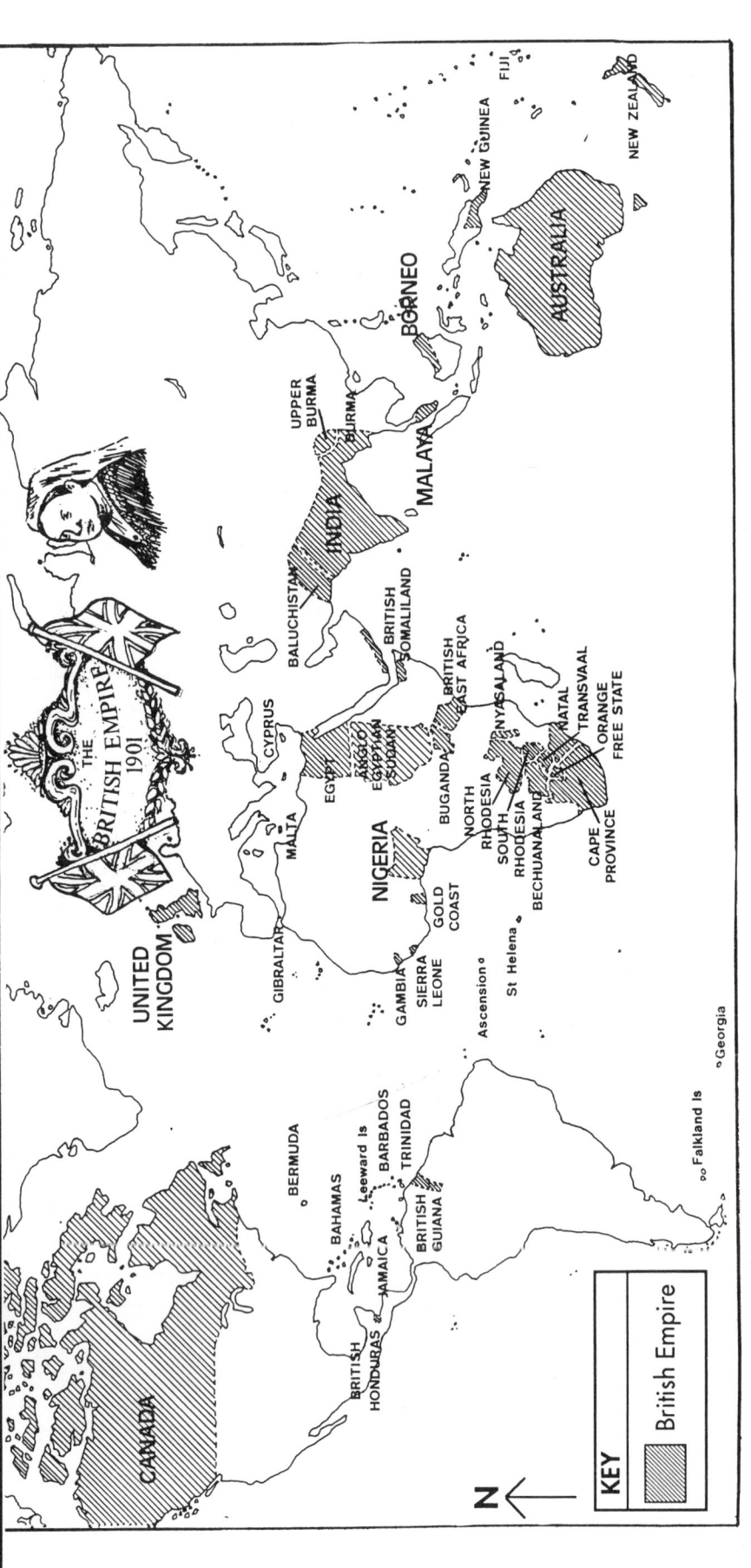

The Sun Never Sets ...

The British Empire 1901		
Colony	Country's name today	Capital today

The British Empire grew throughout Queen Victoria's reign. In 1901 it covered about one quarter of the world's surface. A large army and navy helped to make sure that the colonies remained loyal to the Queen. Gradually each country gained its independence.

- Why do you think people would say that the 'Sun never sets on the British Empire'?
- Why was Britain so keen to have a large Empire?
- Make a chart like this one listing each of Britain's colonies, what it is called now and its capital. You will need an atlas.

The Victoria Line

This picture shows Queen Victoria, Albert and their children in 1857.

PRINCE ALBERT   QUEEN VICTORIA

- Do some research and fill in the missing information about Victoria and Albert. Then use the information below to work out who's who. Label the picture.

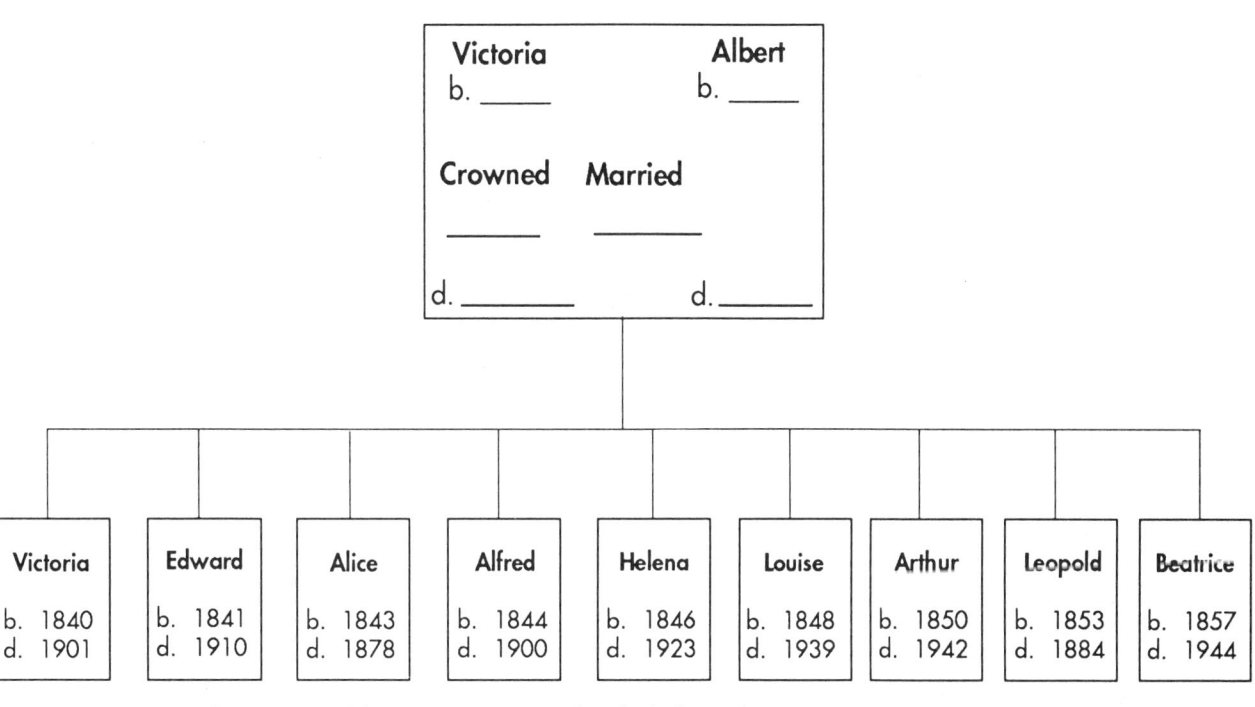

	Victoria	Albert
b.	_____	_____
Crowned	_____	Married _____
d.	_____	_____

Victoria	Edward	Alice	Alfred	Helena	Louise	Arthur	Leopold	Beatrice
b. 1840	b. 1841	b. 1843	b. 1844	b. 1846	b. 1848	b. 1850	b. 1853	b. 1857
d. 1901	d. 1910	d. 1878	d. 1900	d. 1923	d. 1939	d. 1942	d. 1884	d. 1944

- How many boys and how many girls did they have?
- Which child lived to be 92 years old?
- Who was next in line to the throne?
- Who became the next monarch? Why?
- Draw a 'family tree' for your family. Start with your mum and dad and then underneath, enter yourself, your brothers and sisters. Add birth dates for everyone.

© Folens Ltd.   This page may be photocopied for classroom use only

Generation Game

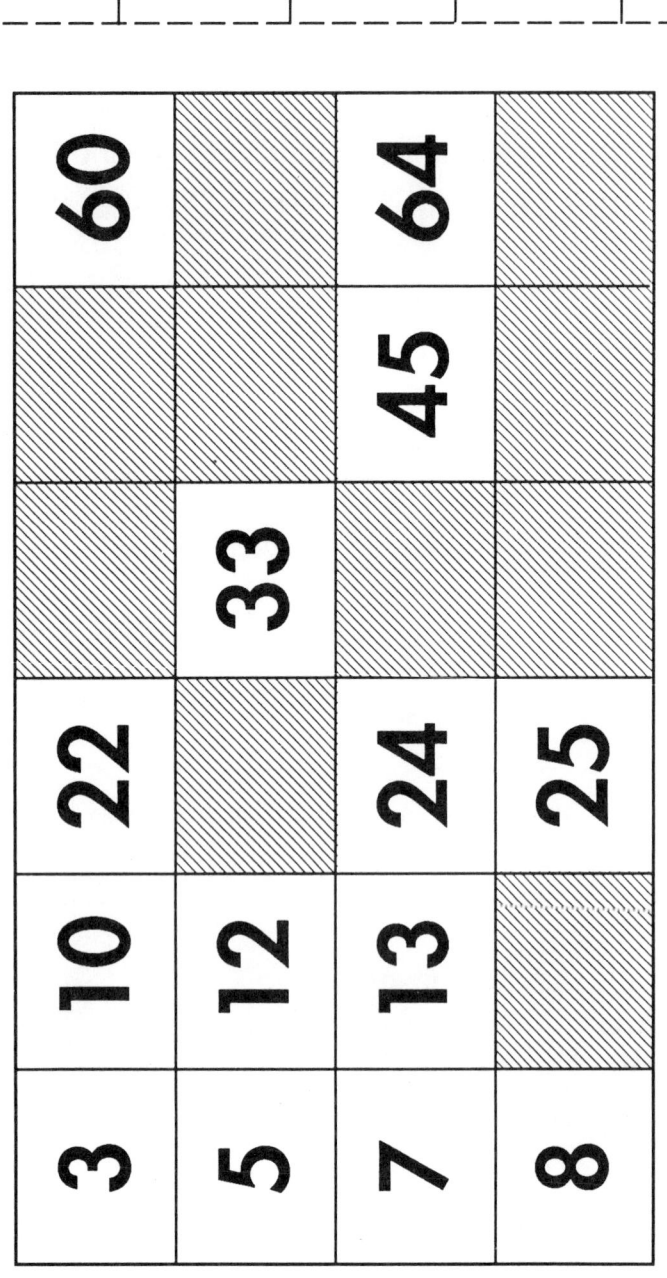

Kings and Queens strips

William III 1694-1702	William III & Mary II 1689-1694	James II 1685-1688	Charles II 1660-1685	Charles I 1625-1649	James I 1603-1625	Elizabeth I 1558-1603

Victoria 1837-1901	William IV 1830-1837	George IV 1820-1830	George III 1760-1820	George II 1727-1760	George I 1714-1727	Anne 1702-1714

3	10	22				60
5	12		33		45	
7	13	24				64
8		25				

- Cut out the Kings and Queens strips and colour them differently.
- Work out how long each King or Queen reigned then cover the correct number on the card with their picture.
- Race your partner. When you have finished shout 'Victoria' to show that you have won.

• How many more years did Queen Victoria reign than:
  - Charles II
  - Elizabeth I
  - George I?

• Make a coloured picture square of Queen Elizabeth II. Find out how long she has been Queen. Write the number on the card in the correct place and cover this square on the card.

Great Victorians

Many now famous people lived in the reign of Queen Victoria (1837-1901).
- Use a history book or encyclopedia to match the person with the invention, discovery, book or work. Write a few sentences about how each affected people's lives and why they are remembered today.

Early steam engine

Florence Nightingale

Origin of Species

Dr Barnardo

First telephone

George Stephenson

David Livingstone

Charles Darwin

Hospital in Crimean War

Oliver Twist

Africa

Charles Dickens

Alexander Graham Bell

Homeless orphans

Folens Ltd.   This page may be photocopied for classroom use only   Page 9

When I'm Sixty-four

VICTORIA BECOMES QUEEN 1837	1838	1839	Queen Victoria marries Albert 1840 >2 Postal service starts	1841	1842	1843	1844
S.S. Great Britain sails 1845 >1	1846	1847	Great authors 1848 >1	1849	1850	Great Exhibition Britain - workshop of the world 1851 >2	Britain - cholera epidemic <2 1852
1853	Crimean War begins <4 1854	1855	Crimean War ends 1856 >3	Indian Mutiny <2 1857	1858	1859	1860
Prince Albert dies Go back to 1840 1861	1862	1863	1864	1865	Dr Barnardo opens children's homes 1866 >3	Working men vote 1867 >2	1868
1869	School Boards set up - a boost for education 1870 >2	1871	Secret voting 1872 >1	Britain now in a serious economic crisis <4 1873	1874	Reforms in health, homes, chimney sweeps 1875 >3	1876
1877	1878	Electric light invented 1879 >2	1880	1881	Cricket England v Australia began 1882 >1	1883	1884
Khartoum falls - General Gordon dies <2 1885	1886	Golden Jubilee 1887 >3	1888	London dockers went on strike <1 1889	1890	Wireless telegraph developed 1891 >1	1892
Aspirin introduced 1893 >1	1894	X-Rays discovered 1895 >2	1896	1897	1898	Boer War begins <5 1899	1900

Many things happened in the 64 years of Queen Victoria's reign.
GOOD THINGS = new inventions, discoveries, laws.
BAD THINGS = war, poverty, disease.

QUEEN VICTORIA DIES 1901 THE END

Use the two stamps as counters.
Race your partner. If you land on something good go forward >, something bad go back <.

COLOUR RED    COLOUR BLACK

Turnpikes

In the early part of the nineteenth century the condition of the roads was poor. Tracks were often knee deep in mud in the winter, holes and cart ruts baked hard in the summer. This meant that the roads were dangerous, uncomfortable and slow.

Local companies or 'trusts' built better roads, from stone and pebbles. People paid a 'toll' (or small fee) to use them. These roads were known as **turnpikes**. At the entrance to a **turnpike** lists of tolls were displayed.

LEEDS–HALIFAX TRUST
CHAIN BAR

FIVE HORSES OR MORE	9d
FOUR HORSES	6d
TWO OR MORE HORSES	4d
ONE HORSE AND CART	3d
EVERY EXTRA DRAUGHT HORSE	1/2d
EVERY DROVE OF OXEN	6d UP TO A SCORE
CALVES, HOGS	2 1/2d UP TO A SCORE

EXEMPTIONS FROM PAYMENT: Persons travelling to vote in Parliamentary elections, vehicles carrying gravel, or road material for the turnpikes, vehicles carrying farm produce and implements in the normal course of husbandry and churchgoers.

J. P. SUTCLIFFE

HOW MUCH DO THESE PEOPLE HAVE TO PAY?

- How much did the tollgate keeper collect in shillings and pence? (12d = 1 shilling)
- Why do you think that 'pikes' or 'spikes' were placed on some gates?
- Do you think that turnpikes were popular with everyone?

Canals

Turnpike roads were expensive to use and only good for carrying light loads quickly. A horse could pull about 4 tonnes by cart but 50 tonnes by barge! Rivers had been used to transport cargo but often they had a strong current and did not always flow to where they were needed. Canals were straighter, had no current and joined towns together.

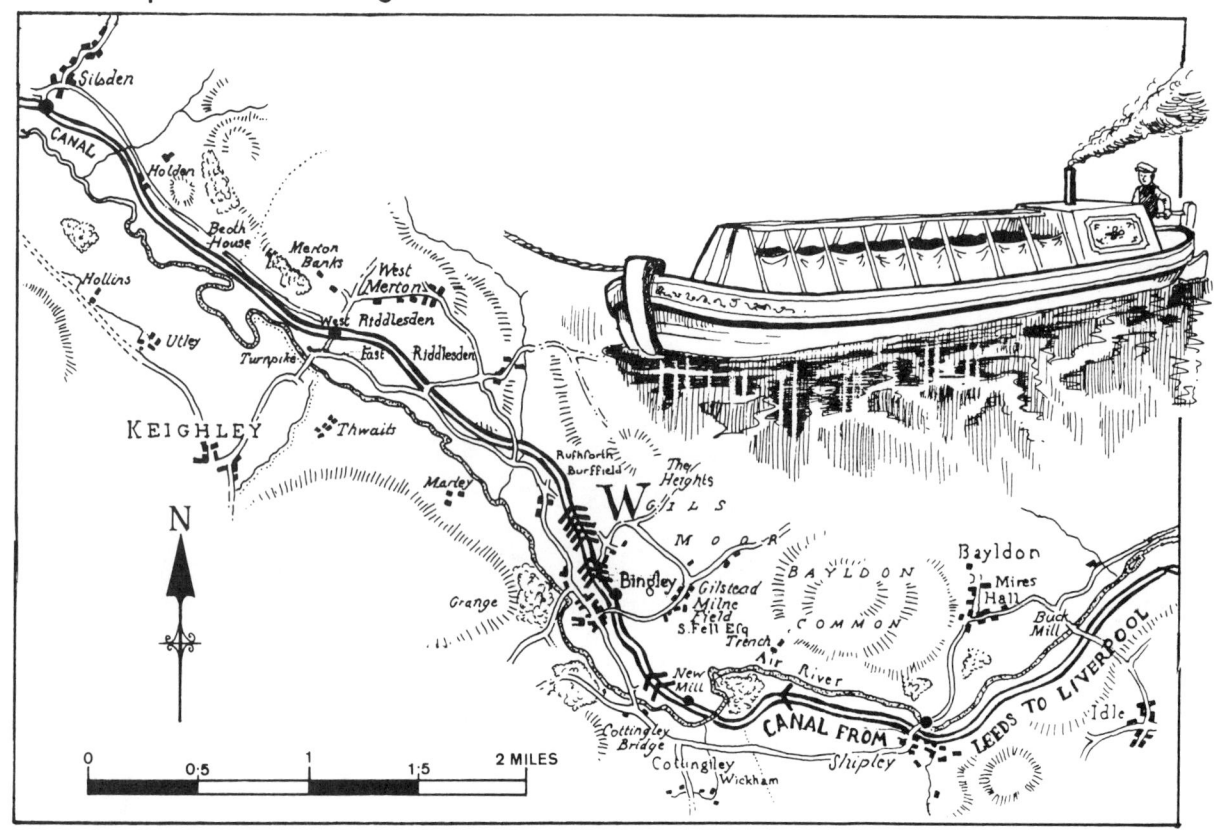

Key
- Lock
- Canal
- Roads
- Hills

- Use a strip of paper to work out the distance from Silsden to Buck Mill by canal.

A horse could pull a barge at about 3 miles (5km) per hour and take 20 minutes to go through a lock.

Use the old fashioned measurements.

- How many miles was the journey?
- How long would the journey take?
- Which was the slowest part of the journey? Why was this?
- List the problems you think that canal transport may have had.

Journey from

	Time
Silsden ~	6am
West Riddlesden ~	
Bingley ~	
New Mill ~	
Shipley ~	
Buck Mill ~	

Iron Horses

Railways allowed large loads to be moved quickly and cheaply. A journey taking several days by canal would take hours by rail. The most famous railway engineer in the early 1800s was George Stephenson who invented a railway engine called 'The Rocket' and opened the first railway line between Stockton and Darlington in 1825. The real heroes of this new railway age were the 'navvies', workmen who, using only muscle power, hacked out hundreds of tunnels, thousands of bridges and laid 34 000km of track during the reign of Queen Victoria.

- Finish the 'Railway Age' cartoon. Make it as imaginative as you can. Use library books to help you.

'Railway mania' began around 1825. Railways were soon more important than canals or roads.	Navvies (mostly Irish) built the railway lines.	Their working day was long: 6 in the morning to 7 in the evening, 7 days a week, rain or shine.	Wages were low, about 2 shillings a week (10p).
Navvies lived in 'shants' (wooden huts). They were dirty and crowded; disease was common.	They were not welcomed in towns along the line because of drunkenness and fighting.	Navvies did the hardest most dangerous jobs such as using explosives and digging tunnels.	Many died, but because of them factories grew and people could visit places only dreamed of before.

Going Loco

Building a railway was not an easy job. As well as the usual problems of linking towns and keeping the line level, many landowners were unhappy. Some said that their fields would turn black and that cows would stop giving milk, others set their bulls and dogs on the railwaymen to stop them working.

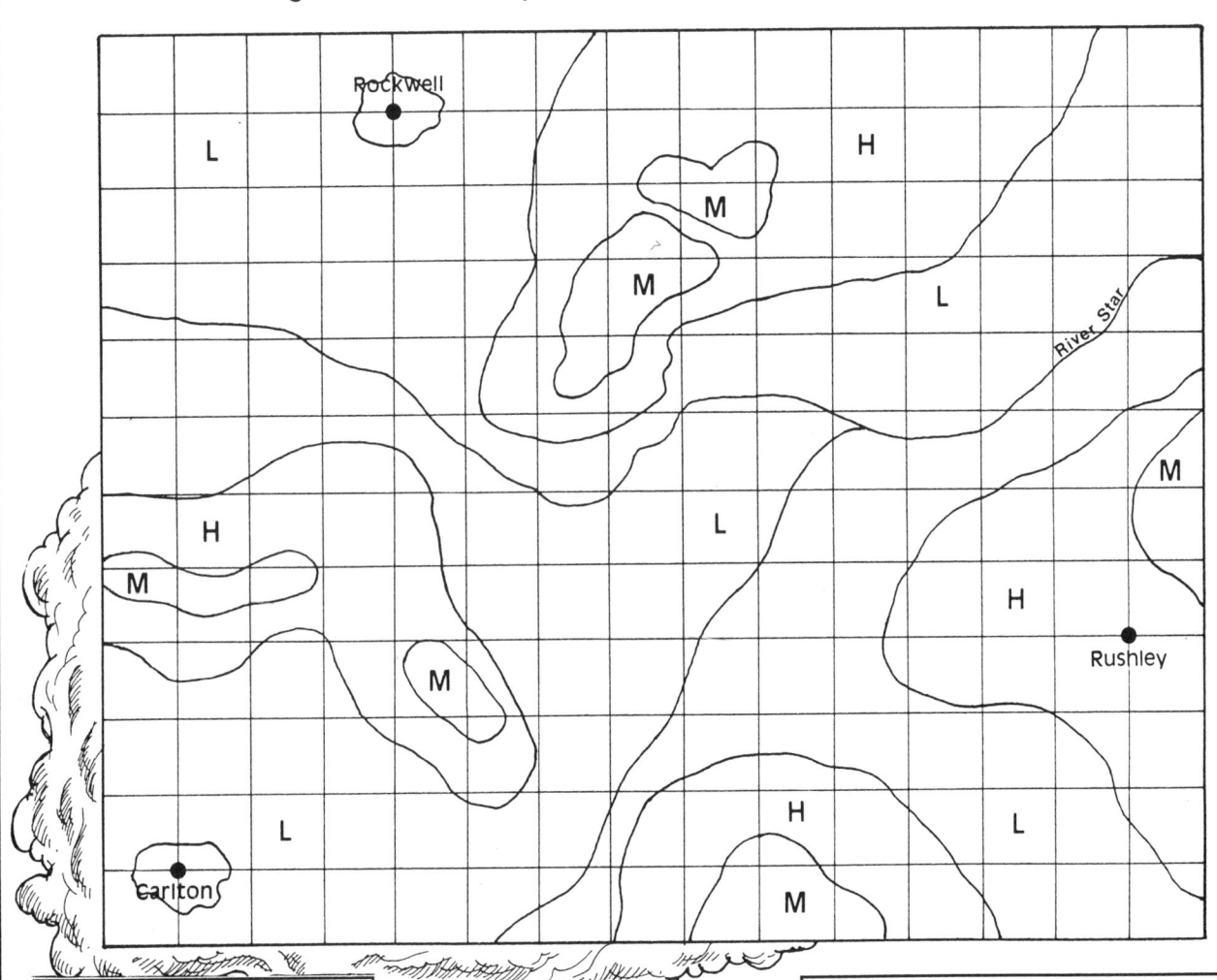

BILL for building a 'RAILWAY LINE'

Track:
Lowland _____
Highland _____
Mountains _____

Total bill _____

Charges

Lowland	L	£1000 a square
Highland	H	£2000 a square
Mountains	M	£3000 a square

● Station towns

If highland and lowland are in the same square use the highest charge.

Plan a railway line to join the towns as cheaply as you can.
- Use different colours to shade the mountains, highland, lowland and town areas and then use the key to work out costs. Total up the bill on the chart.
- List the problems a railway engineer would have when building a new railway line.
- What effect do you think the new railways had on the lives of people in these towns?

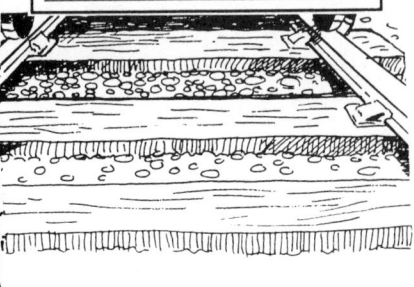

Takes Your Breath Away

TO THE NOBILITY & GENTRY
MAY 1896

THE GREAT HORSELESS CARRIAGE Co. Ltd

HAS THE HONOUR TO PRESENT

This NOVEL vehicle is propelled by an **INTERNAL COMBUSTION ENGINE** OF 2 CYLINDERS AND 6 HORSE POWER relying on petroleum for its motive force. THE MECHANICAL carriage will attain the comfortable speed of **TWELVE MILES PER HOUR** on the level, while hills can be ascended and descended in safety.

The Daimler Wagonette is admirably suited to the needs of the **SPORTSMAN** AND LOVER OF THE COUNTRYSIDE, giving as it does full facilities for the enjoyment of PRESH AIR AND AN UNINTERRUPTED VIEW OF THE Scenery.

'A new mode of transport that has undoubtedly come to stay' — THE DAILY PRESS

THE TWIN-CYLINDER 6 H.P. WAGONETTE {See Engraving}

"THINKING OF BUYING A NEW CAR, SIR?"

At the end of the century Karl Benz invented a new way of travelling, the petrol driven car (known as the 'horseless carriage'). Advertisements at the time compared the advantages of the 'horseless carriage' to the disadvantages of the horse.

- Use the advertisement. In the speech balloons, write six ways that cars were better than horses.
- What do you think 'horse power' means? Find out if we still use this term today.

Workshop Of The World

Time	John's day	My day
5am		
6am		
7am		
8am		
9am		
10am		
11am		
12 noon		
1pm		
2pm		
3pm		
4pm		
5pm		
6pm		
7pm		
8pm		
9pm		

Over 100 years ago goods made in British factories were wanted all over the world.

Factory owners grew rich but they kept their workers poor. Children, often as young as 5 years old, had to go out to work. Mill owners wanted to employ children because they needed to pay them only half as much as a man.

This is how John described his working day.

> 'We had to be up at 5 in the morning to get to the factory, ready to begin work at 6, then work while 8, when we stopped half an hour for breakfast, then work to 12 noon; for dinner we had 1 hour, then work while 4. We then had half an hour for tee, if anything was left, then commenced work again to 8.30. If any time during the day had been lost, we had to work while 9 o'clock, and so on every night until it was all made up.'
>
> 1864

- Write a word in each space next to the time, saying what John is doing during his working day.
- How does the length of this working day compare with yours at school? Fill in the space for your day.

The hours were long. Life at the mill was not easy. Factory owners were often cruel.

Grimethorpe Mill Rules

1 - No sitting down.
2 - No opening a window.
3 - No looking out of a window.
4 - No running.
5 - No whistling.

- Give a reason why a factory owner might have each rule.

The Price Of Coal

Lord Shaftesbury and many others were ashamed that children were being forced to work long hours in cruel conditions. He received many reports on conditions in factories and mines and about chimney sweeps.

Doctor's Report
The list of those poor children injured or killed at Grimethorpe Mill is long indeed.
This week alone I must add -
Robert Shaw - hair caught in a machine - scalped
Tom Hudson - caught in a machine - hand crushed
Hannah Greenwood - fell into a loom - killed.
1849

John Saville Aged 7
I am usually in the dark and sit down near the door. I'm down the pit for 12 hours a day. I only see daylight on Sundays. One day I fell asleep and a wagon ran over my leg.
1849

London Sweeps
Five or six year olds are the best because they're little. After work their arms and legs are bleeding so I rub them with salt-water before sending them up another chimney.
Sweep Master.
1850

I never got stuck myself but some did and were taken out dead. They were smothered for want of air and the fright from being there so long.
Joseph aged 9
1849

- Write a report on the work of children for Lord Shaftesbury to use in Parliament.
- Describe each job shown above and say why you think it is wrong.

You Rang M'Lord 1

Many people worked 'in service' as servants to wealthy people. Towards the end of Queen Victoria's reign over two million people worked as servants. Although they were not well paid, working conditions were much better than in the mines or mills. Read the information on 'You Rang M'Lord 2'.

- Match the servant with the job they do on these two sheets.
- Read the information, cut out the picture and paste it in the correct frame.

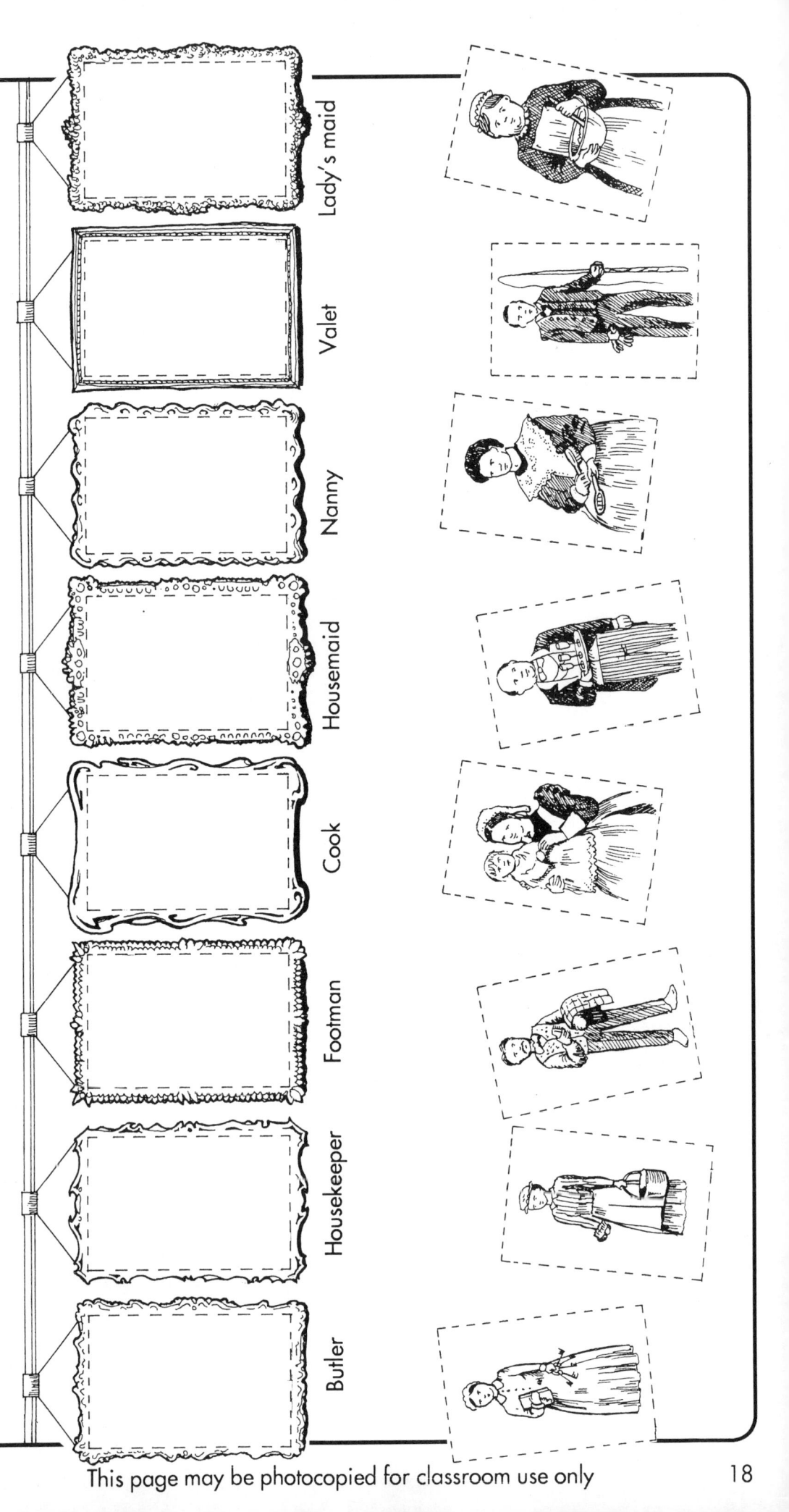

Lady's maid

Valet

Nanny

Housemaid

Cook

Footman

Housekeeper

Butler

You Rang M'Lord 2

- Identify the servant. Write the correct name in the job description.

Housekeeper   Housemaid   Valet   Nanny   Butler   Lady's maid   Footman   Cook

Situation
- carry the coals
- clean and polish the boots
- cleaning cutlery
- ride on the carriage
- wait at table

£12-20 a year

Situation
- in charge of the children and babies
- in charge of the nursery maids

£15-30 a year

Situation
- care for the master's clothes
- take care of travel arrangements
- advise on matters of politeness
- be a 'gentleman's gentleman'

£12-20 a year

Situation
- must be young and strong
- cleaning the house
- do all the washing
- light the kitchen range
- light all the fires

£12-20 a year

Situation
- trustworthy and honest
- discipline the staff
- answer the door
- bring in breakfast
- look after the wine cellar
- wait at table
- iron the newspapers

£30-50 a year

Situation
- engage and dismiss maids
- give out cleaning materials
- book-keeping
- buy household items
- control female servants

£20-45 a year

Situation
- produce menus for large dinner parties
- do all the shopping for food
- be in charge of the scullery maids

£14-30 a year

Situation
- have good manners, young and cheerful
- care for her mistress's clothes and appearance
- look after the dressing room

£12-25 a year

Street Directories

A good way of finding out about jobs in the past is to look at 'Street Directories'. These list the people living in each house, street by street and tell you their occupation.
- Look at this part of an 1878 directory.

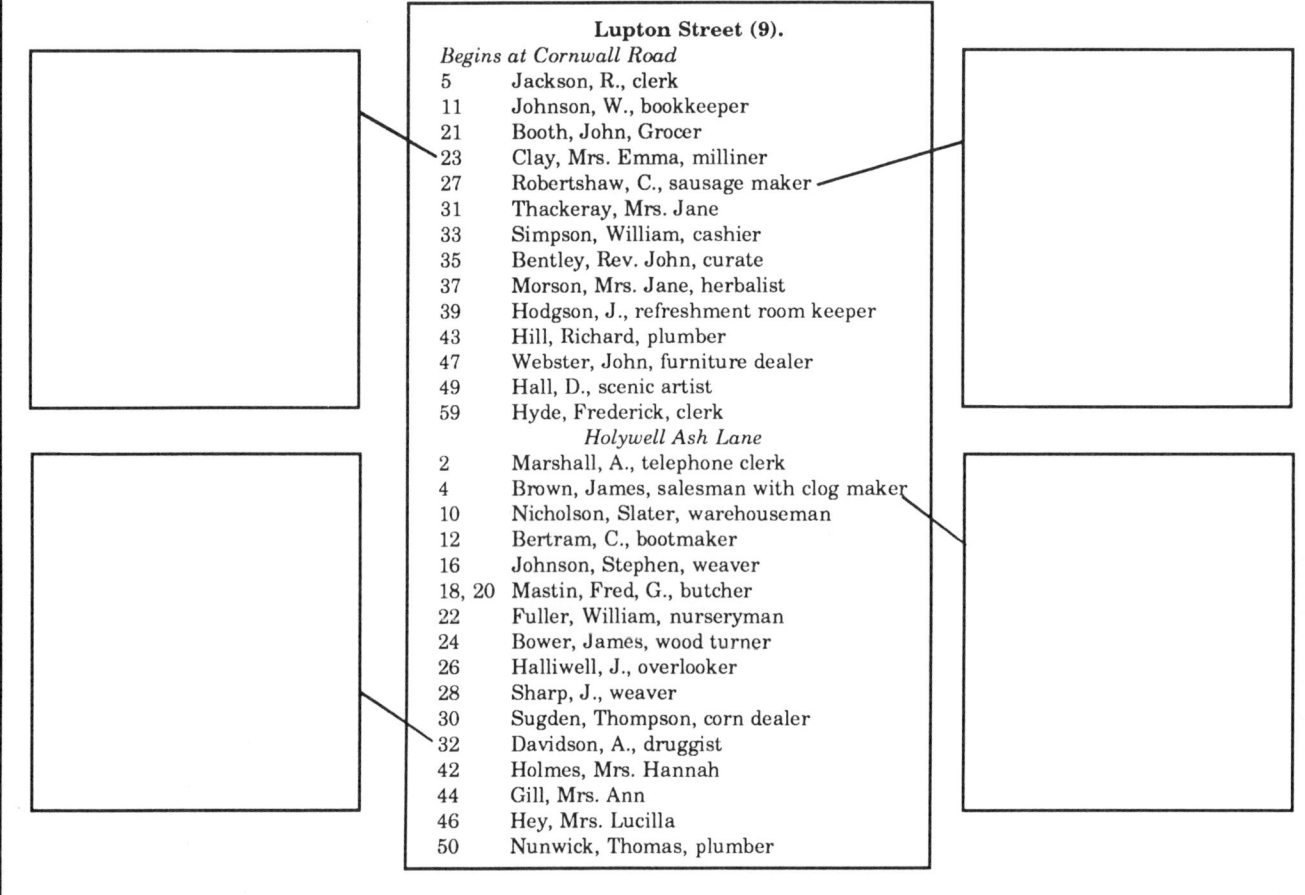

Lupton Street (9).
Begins at Cornwall Road
5	Jackson, R., clerk
11	Johnson, W., bookkeeper
21	Booth, John, Grocer
23	Clay, Mrs. Emma, milliner
27	Robertshaw, C., sausage maker
31	Thackeray, Mrs. Jane
33	Simpson, William, cashier
35	Bentley, Rev. John, curate
37	Morson, Mrs. Jane, herbalist
39	Hodgson, J., refreshment room keeper
43	Hill, Richard, plumber
47	Webster, John, furniture dealer
49	Hall, D., scenic artist
59	Hyde, Frederick, clerk

Holywell Ash Lane
2	Marshall, A., telephone clerk
4	Brown, James, salesman with clog maker
10	Nicholson, Slater, warehouseman
12	Bertram, C., bootmaker
16	Johnson, Stephen, weaver
18, 20	Mastin, Fred, G., butcher
22	Fuller, William, nurseryman
24	Bower, James, wood turner
26	Halliwell, J., overlooker
28	Sharp, J., weaver
30	Sugden, Thompson, corn dealer
32	Davidson, A., druggist
42	Holmes, Mrs. Hannah
44	Gill, Mrs. Ann
46	Hey, Mrs. Lucilla
50	Nunwick, Thomas, plumber

- Look at the four jobs pointed to. Write the name of each job in the correct box and draw a picture.

Look at the directory and make a graph. The first one has been done for you.
- What area do most people work in?
- Which jobs would you not find today?

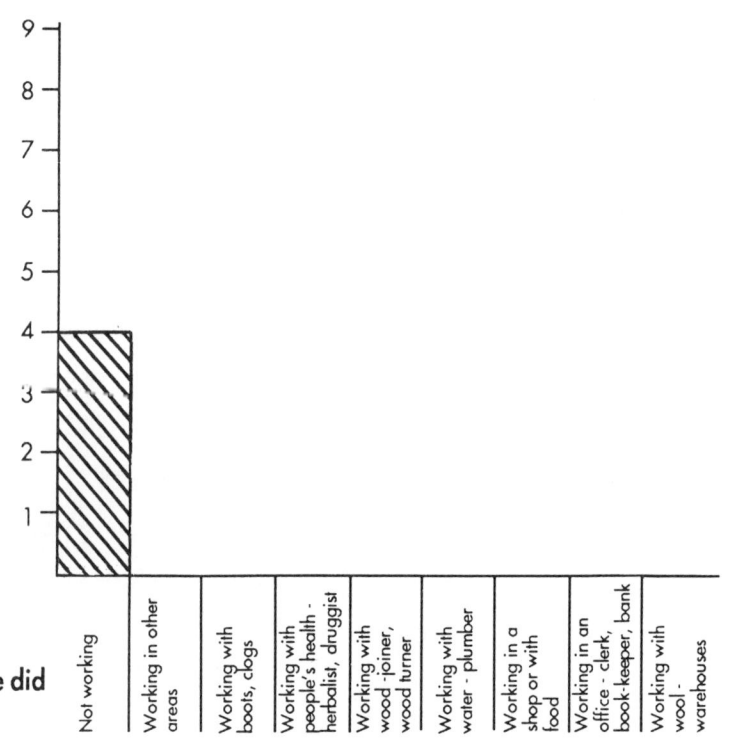

Graph to show jobs people did in Lupton Street 1878

Categories (x-axis):
- Not working
- Working in other areas
- Working with boots, clogs
- Working with people's health - herbalist, druggist
- Working with wood - joiner, wood turner
- Working with water - plumber
- Working in a shop or with food
- Working in an office - clerk, book-keeper, bank
- Working with wool - warehouses

"Not working" column filled to 4.

Plough The Fields And Scatter

Until about 1850 most people in Britain lived in the countryside and worked on farms for local landowners. Wages were very poor and life was hard but it was better and healthier than in the towns. Everyone helped to work on the land, even the children.

- Find the words in the the word search to complete the jobs children had to do.

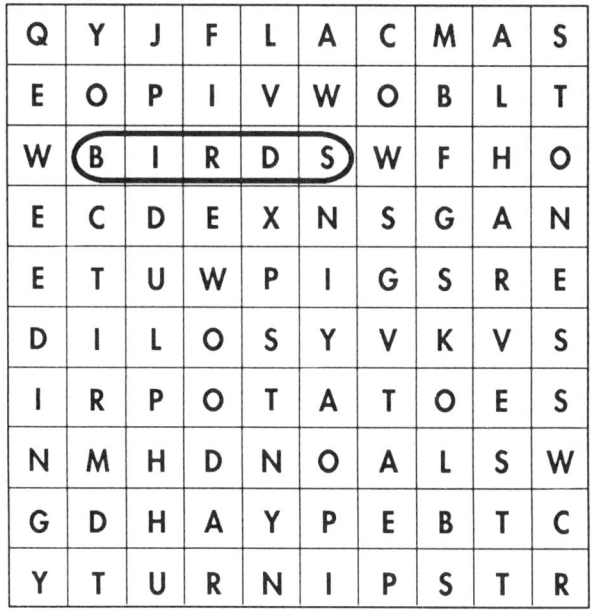

SCARING _ _ _ _ _

HELPING WITH THE _ _ _ _ _ _

PLANTING _ _ _ _ _ _ _

MAKING _ _ _

PICKING UP _ _ _ _ _ _

Q	Y	J	F	L	A	C	M	A	S
E	O	P	I	V	W	O	B	L	T
W	B	I	R	D	S	W	F	H	O
E	C	D	E	X	N	S	G	A	N
E	T	U	W	P	I	G	S	R	E
D	I	L	O	S	Y	V	K	V	S
I	R	P	O	T	A	T	O	E	S
N	M	H	D	N	O	A	L	S	W
G	D	H	A	Y	P	E	B	T	C
Y	T	U	R	N	I	P	S	T	R

COLLECTING _ _ _ _ _ _ _ _

LOOKING AFTER _ _ _ _

CLEANING _ _ _ _ _ _

HERDING _ _ _ _

_ _ _ _ _ _ THE CORN

- Make a word search about working and living in the countryside or town in Victorian Britain.
- What happened to the land workers after 1850 when new agricultural machinery was introduced?

Where There's Muck

Victorian towns were unhealthy. Living conditions for the poor were especially bad with open sewers, shared privies (toilets), badly made houses and crowded streets.

- Read these four descriptions written about part of a West Yorkshire town in 1849.

1. Gaugers Croft
... here I found a cellar dwelling of two rooms, one was a wool combers shop the other a living room and kitchen in which sleeps 7 in two beds. It is unbearably hot during the day and night a high temperature being needed to comb the wool. Disease is common here.

2. Main Street
... into the midden steads is thrown household refuse and offal from the slaughter house. It is mixed with night soil and pig sty waste and lies exposed for months giving out foul smells and gases.

3. Newall Hill
... I found 7 houses in front of Newall Hill without any privy. I found 24 houses in the main street with only one privy between them.

4. Spring Head
... the water in this well is used by many people, it is often bad and sometimes so green and putrid that cattle refuse to drink it.

Night soil carriers

- Find out what these five words mean: cellar, offal, midden steads, night soil, putrid.
- What do you think the health of people in this town was like?

PUBLIC NOTICE

TO THE RESIDENTS OF HAWORTH, WEST YORKSHIRE

The following rules must be observed to improve the health of the town ~

1 ~

2 ~

3 ~

4 ~

BOARD OF HEALTH - HAWORTH 1849

- Make up four rules to help improve the health of local people in 1849.

Fatal Diseases

In early Victorian Britain people died of diseases which are virtually unheard of today. Hospitals were dangerous places. They were dirty, overcrowded and their nurses untrained. Patients were strapped to a table or made drunk before an operation. In the middle of the nineteenth century anaesthetics were discovered and doctors knew clean tools and surroundings were important.

cholera

tuberculosis

The patient's face has swollen and is turning black, he smells. He has a high temperature and fever.

This patient is a young child. The disease is leaving scars on his face and he may go blind.

This patient has great problems breathing and is slowly wasting away. He coughs loudly, very often.

The patient has cramps and turns blue; he is sick all the time. He has the most dreadful diarrhoea.

Do some research

typhus

smallpox

- Read the symptoms of each patient carefully and then try to find out which of the four diseases each has. Write your answer at the bottom of each chart.
- Why did people catch these diseases so easily in the nineteenth century?
- Why are they rarely heard of today?

In Loving Memory

Look at the two letters from Mrs Skelton to Miss Thorpe the headteacher.

> Mrs Skelton,
> 16 Hird St
> Shipley.
>
> To Miss Thorpe
> I am writing to tell you that Emma Skelton cannot come to school at Present untill I get my Home stoved as her Sister Eva died 3 weeks ago. I think you would know her as she was one of your scholars she died with tuberculosis and I lost my other daughter Hannah last tuesday and buried only Friday so I do not wish to spread any decease about the school children as Im sure there has been quite plenty of illness amongst children I'm exspecting my Home disinficting and as soon as all is cleared away Emma will come Back Ive buried 2 of my Daughters in 3 weeks and I'm sure its Plenty of trouble and I dont want to lose any more so for safety for my child and also the school children I think its best for Emma to stay at Home untill all is over.
> I remain
> yours Truly
> Mrs Skelton

> Miss Thorpe
> Head Mistress
> Saltaire Central School
> Shipley

~ 2 weeks later ~

> 16 Hird St,
> Shipley.
>
> Dear Miss Thorpe
> We regret to inform you that Emma Skelton is to ill to come to school. She has been ordered to the seaside for a change of air so we are going to take her to Saltburn for a week or two. She will come back to school when she is better.
> yours truly,
> Mrs Skelton

1895

Many children died young. Victorian families were often big in order that some of the children would grow up and become adults. Families with over eight children were common.

- Why is Mrs Skelton getting her house 'stoved'?
- How many of her children have died?
- What do you think is the matter with Emma?
- Who has ordered Emma to go away? Is this a good idea?
- Although there are a number of mistakes in the letter do you think that Mrs Skelton is well educated?

At Rest

The increase in population in Victorian Britain combined with a high death rate meant that large cemeteries had to be built. Wealthy Victorians built large impressive gravestones as monuments to themselves. Gravestones of the poor were usually simple stones with little carved on them.

Burials	Age at death
Mary Child	44 years
Harnet Kellet	1 and a half years
Leah Elizabeth Fox	9 weeks
Squire Thorp	9 months
Timothy Mitchell	86 years
Deborah Barker	66 years
Martha Taylor	4 years
Sarah Ann Hunton	6 years
Hannah Wardwas	74 years
Joshua Hird	4 years
Hannah Nowerth	18 years
Abraham Haley	77 years
Mary Haley	83 years
James Brown	3 and a half years
Esther Wilkinson	61 years
Jane Babes	6 months
Sarah Jackson	5 years
Matthew Crabtree	50 years
Richard Hy. Blakeborough	8 months
George Broadbent	5 days
Bryan Ingham	3 years
Thos. Wardman	6 months
John Sugden	7 and a half years
Hannah Hillman	9 months
Margaret Clayton	4 years
Hannah Armstrong	13 years
Charles Baldwin	4 months
Edward Sidebottom	9 months
Elizabeth Dean	9 weeks
Sarah Parker	80 years
Hannah Mitchell	73 years
Ann Harthington	60 years
Margaret Greenwood	10 years
Sarah Barraclough	20 years
May Franklin	4 months
Elizabeth Prestley	28 years
Hannah Turner	3 years
Sevi Frankland	11 months
Thomas Cartmall	11 years
Amos Pollard	4 years
Elizabeth Smith	10 years
Mary Haley	1 year
Sarah Bargeburg	14 weeks
Ann Popplewell	2 years
Robert Popplewell	12 days
Susannah Thornton	13 months
William Roberts	26 years
Benjamin Turner	13 years
John Thornton	79 years
Mary Kershaw	18 years
Mary Watmough	7 years
James Priestley	53 years
Martha Storey	77 years
Grace Wolfenden	7 years

This is a list of names and ages at death taken from a Victorian cemetery. From it make a tally |||| and draw a bar graph.

0 - 1 yr	1 - 5 yrs	6 - 10 yrs	11 - 20 yrs
21 - 30 yrs	31 - 40 yrs	41 - 50 yrs	over 51

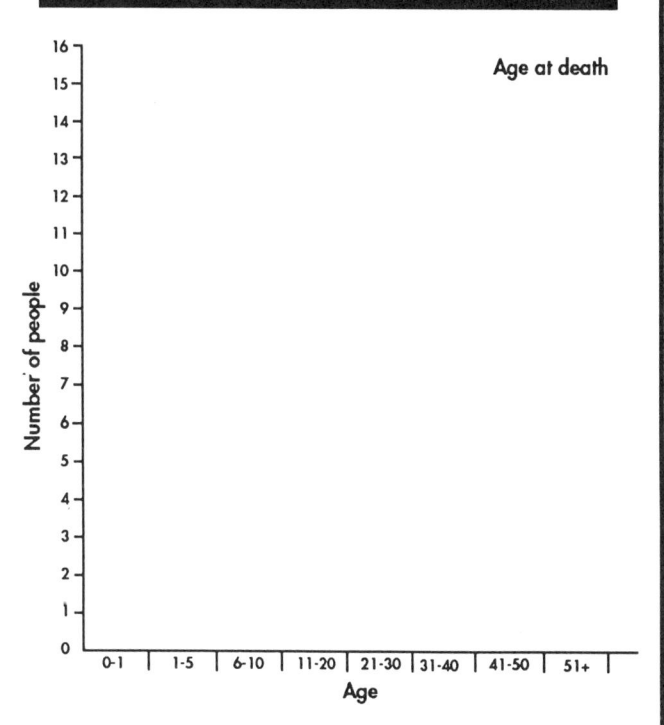

- At what age were most deaths?
- Between which years were the fewest deaths?
- Calculate the average age of death for men and women.
- Look at the names. List any that you would not hear today.
- Conduct a survey yourself at a local Victorian cemetery. How do your results compare?

Sunday

In Victorian times Sunday was a special day, the Lord's Day. Nearly everyone went to church on Sunday, often more than once. Children could not play with toys, they could read, but only the Bible. All the shops and entertainments were closed. Look at Joseph's Sunday.

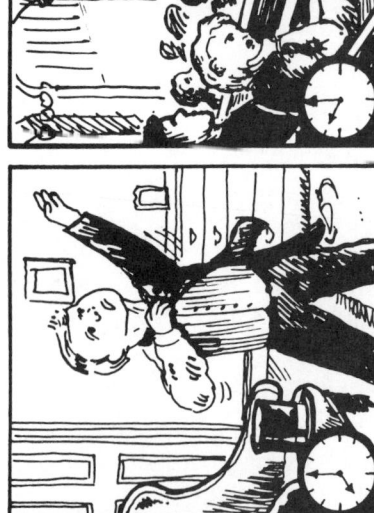

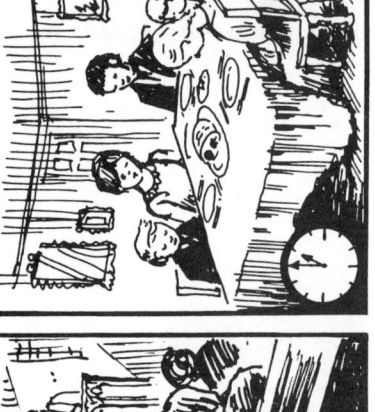

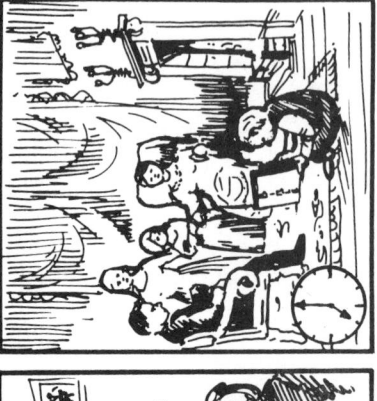

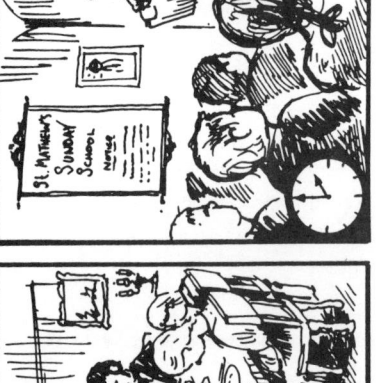

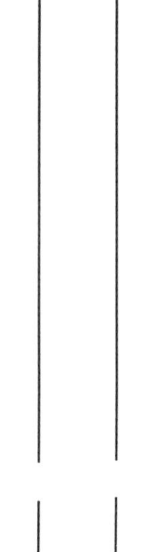

- Describe what is happening in each picture, and why.
- Draw your own 'Picture Sunday' showing what happens at each of these times. How does your Sunday compare with Joseph's?
- Over 100 years ago most people were Christians: members of the Church of England, Roman Catholics, Methodists, Baptists and Quakers. Conduct a survey in your class. Are there any different religions?

© Folens Ltd. This page may be photocopied for classroom use only

Brave New World

By the end of Queen Victoria's reign people could expect a healthier and longer life because of improvements in medicine and public health.
- The pictures and captions are all mixed up. Cut out the pictures and the captions and match them up. Paste the correct pairs on a strip of paper.
- Do some research and find out when each improvement shown in the picture happened. Look carefully at each picture to find a clue.

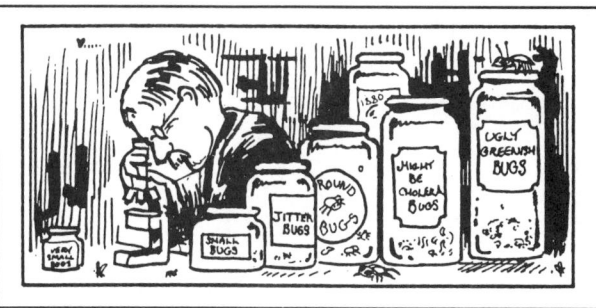

Eberth discovered the germs that caused typhoid. Later Koch discovered the cholera germ.	An Act of Parliament made sure councils supplied pure drinking water and covered drains and sewers.
Simpson invented chloroform for use during operations. Up to this time patients were strapped down or made drunk before being operated on.	Florence Nightingale changed attitudes towards nursing after the Crimean War. The first nursing school opened in England as a result.
The General Medical Council was formed to raise standards and train doctors.	Inside toilets were becoming popular with richer people. Still too expensive for poorer people to afford.
Public Health Reports by Edwin Chadwick made Parliament instruct councils to clean up towns.	By 1900 injections against typhoid were quite common.

© Folens Ltd.

Time Traveller

TIME TRAVELLER
N°6 BRICKYARD
MAY 16th 2487
BY   CHANNEL 74

I'm standing in Brick Yard, a collection of slums where the poor people live. The only entrance is a narrow passage just wide enough for the 'night soil cart' to enter to empty the privies.

PRIVY

Do they look happy? Why not?

Time Traveller is a TV programme of the future.
- Fill in the presenter's reports, colour the sketches then answer his question.

Civic Pride

Britain's towns and cities grew quickly throughout the nineteenth century. More food was being produced, there was more work and families were large. By the end of Queen Victoria's reign over half the population lived in towns.

1801			1901
20 000	Belfast		350 000
13 000	Bradford		230 000
2 000	Cardiff		164 000
82 000	Liverpool		685 000
75 000	Manchester		645 000

Key: 1801 / 1901

- Fill in the graph showing the increase in population up to 1901. Use the key.
- Which town grew the fastest over this time?

Often there was rivalry between neighbouring towns. Here is the mayor of Telbridge comparing his town to nearby Bradfield.

- WE HAVE 4 TRAINS GOING TO LONDON EACH DAY. THERE ARE ONLY 2 FROM BRADFIELD.
- TELBRIDGE IS FULL OF HAPPY, HEALTHY PEOPLE.
- OUR CANAL IS MUCH CLEANER THAN THEIRS.
- OUR TOWN HALL HAS A 200 FOOT TOWER AND I THINK THE BIGGEST CLOCK IN THE NORTH.
- THE PARKS IN TELBRIDGE ARE MUCH MORE PLEASANT THAN THOSE IN BRADFIELD.

- Underline in **green** which of his claims you think are **fact** and underline in **red** which of his claims you think are **points of view**.

Home Sweet Home

Better off Victorians lived in homes which had lots of rooms, for themselves and their servants. They were dry, well built and had large gardens.

- It is June 1885 and the 'Toffs' are moving in to their new home. Label each room using the word box. Say where you would put these pieces of furniture: *grandfather clock, sideboard, large table, dresser for plates, collection of plants.*

WORD BOX
Scullery
Conservatory
Vestibule
Dining Room
Stairs to bedrooms and servants' rooms
Parlour
Stairs to the cellars and wine cellar
Entrance Hall

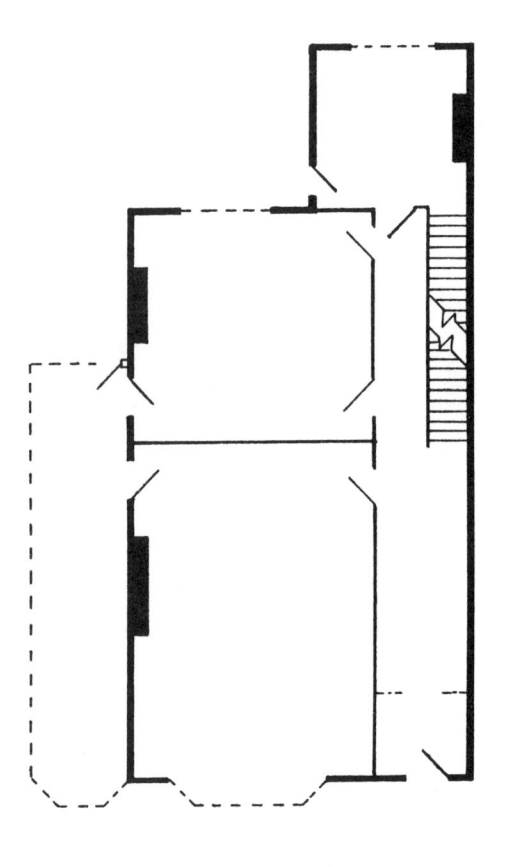

Houses in a poor area - 'back to backs'

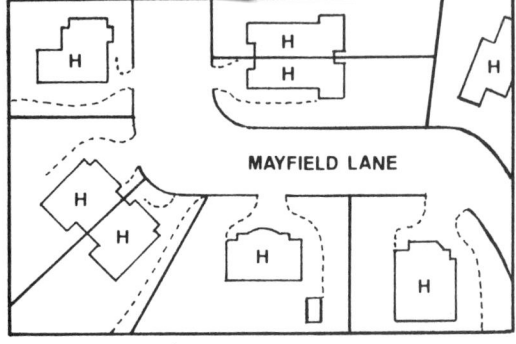

Houses in a richer area

- These two maps show different parts of the same town. Each area is just bigger than a football pitch.
  - How many houses are there in each area?
  - If eight people lived in each house, how many people would live in each area?
- Look at a local map. Are there any street patterns like these to show you where poor areas or rich areas used to be in Victorian times?

© Folens Ltd. This page may be photocopied for classroom use only

Parlour Games 1

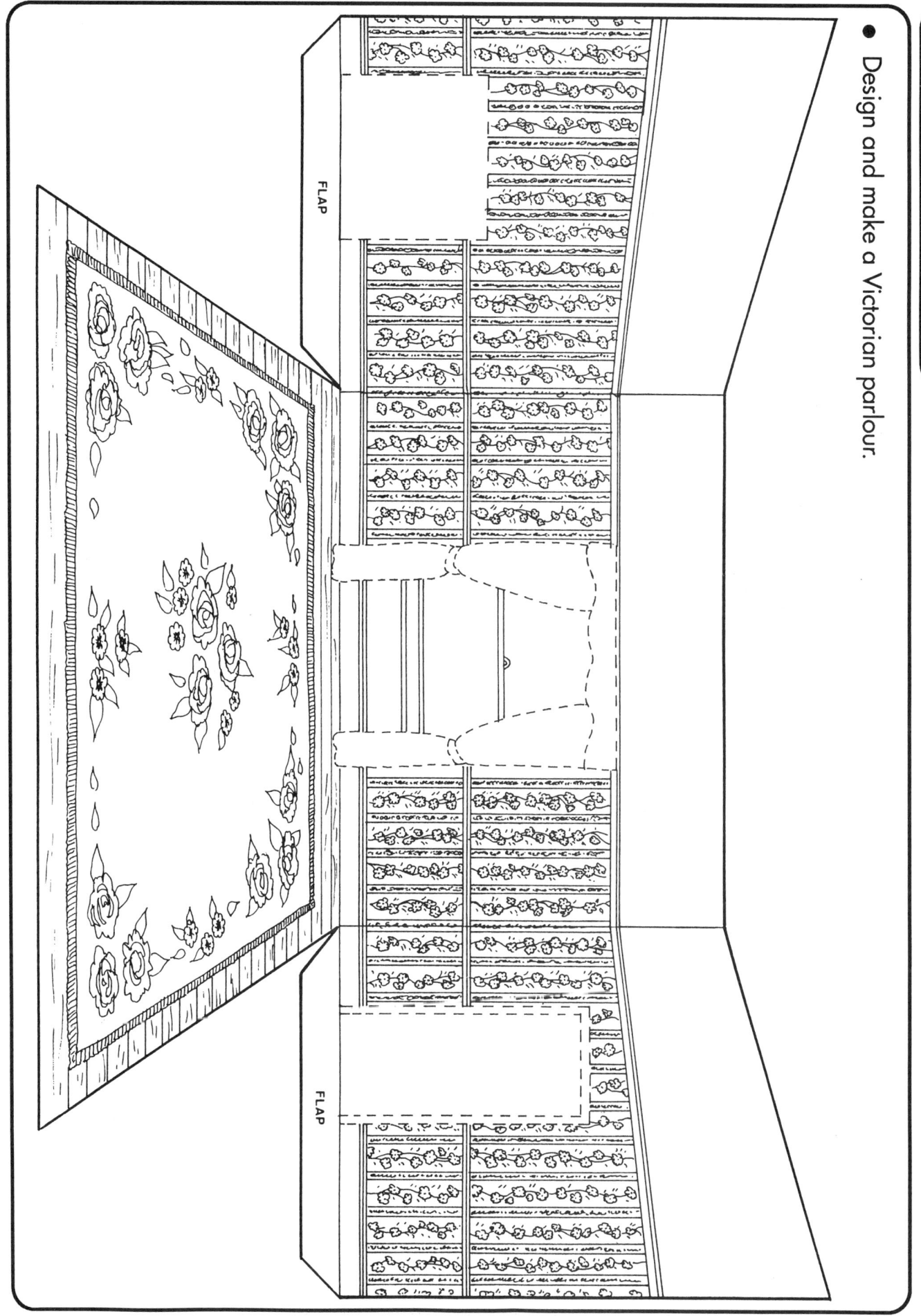

- Design and make a Victorian parlour.

FLAP

FLAP

© Folens Ltd. This page may be photocopied for classroom use only 31

Parlour Games 2

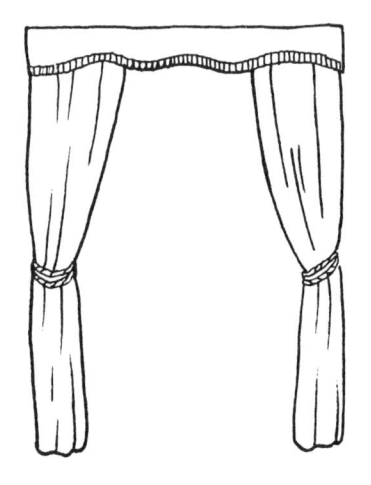

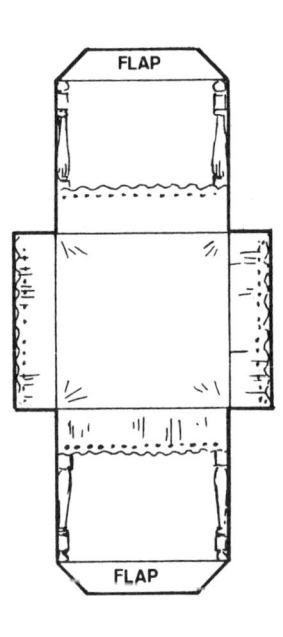

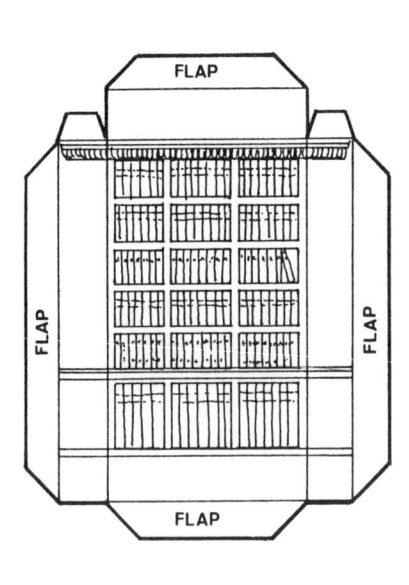

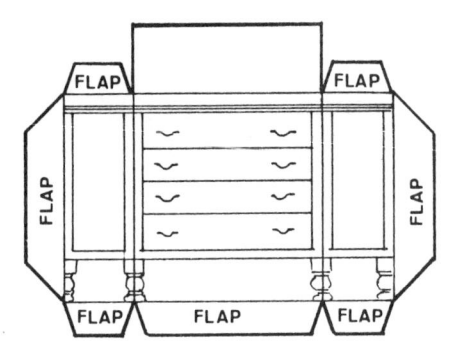

- Cut out the outline in Parlour Games 1.
- Use library books to find out what Victorian furniture looked like and the colours used to decorate rooms.
- Using the information from your research, colour the pictures.
- Cut out the pictures and paste them on to the parlour.
- Score, fold and paste the parlour together. Make a class display and talk about similarities and differences.

Homework

These objects might have been used in a Victorian home.
- Use mail-order catalogues or reference books to find pictures of objects used today to do the same jobs. Draw or paste them into the spaces.
- Write a a few sentences about each object. Consider:
  (a) the job it does
  (b) how technology has changed
  (c) how it has changed people's lives.

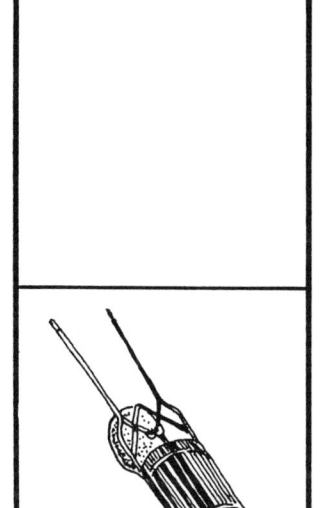

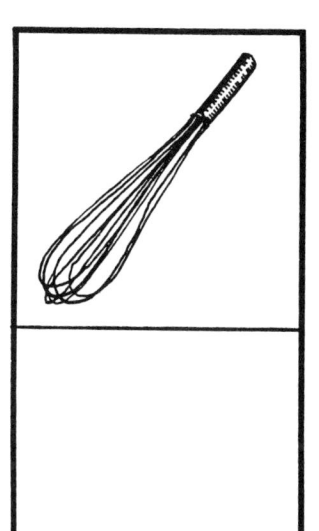

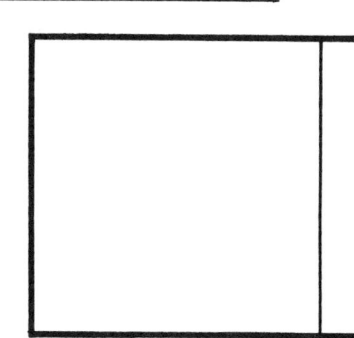

Folens Ltd.   This page may be photocopied for classroom use only   Page 33

Changing Places

Villages were, and still are, different in their layout than towns. People squeezed houses into any spaces unlike in town where they usually formed patterns in streets. The village was a small community and within it was everything the people needed.

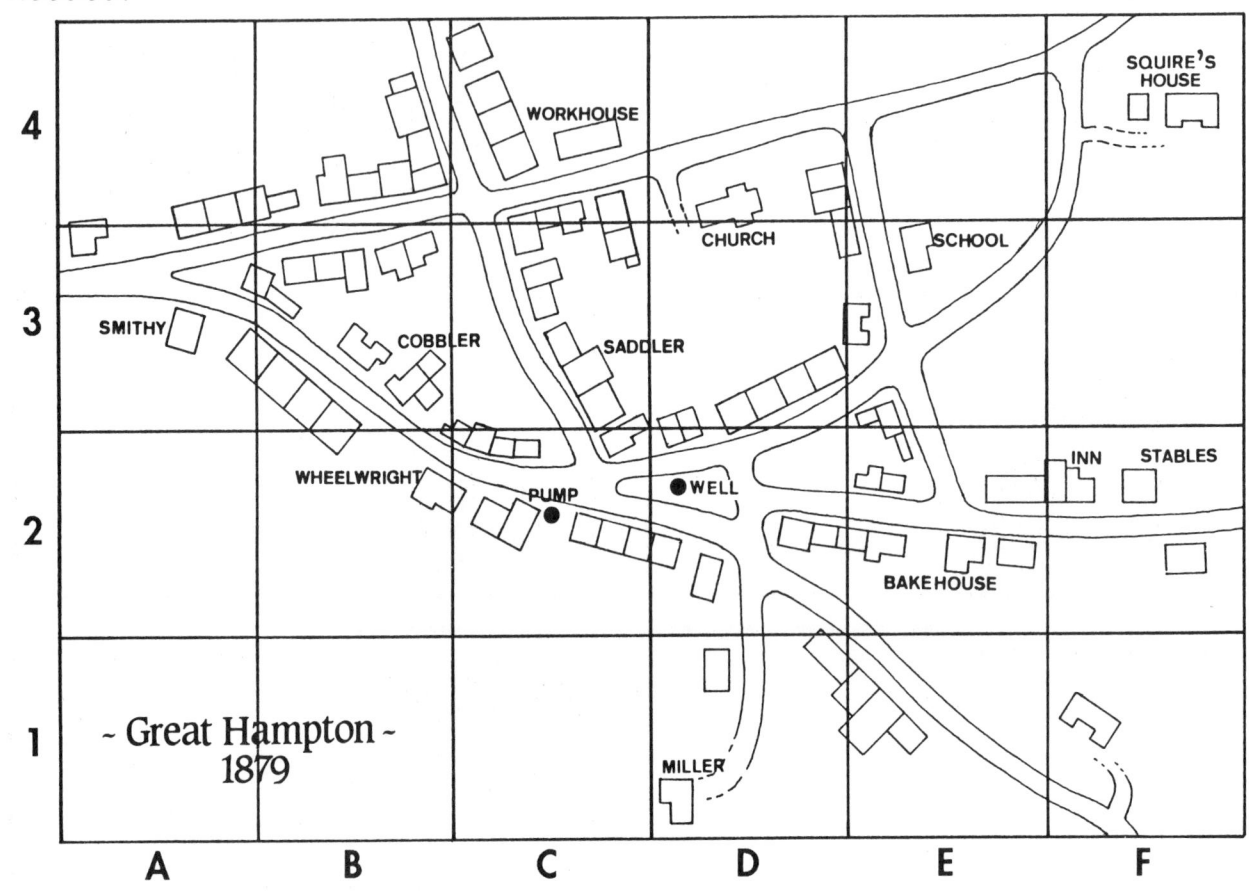

~ Great Hampton ~
1879

- Look carefully at the map. What would you find in a Victorian village that you might not find today?
- Each space in this chart should have a name, grid reference and picture for eight Victorian village activities. Fill in the gaps.

Smithy			Pump	C2		C4
Well		Miller	D1		Stables	

Folens Ltd.   This page may be photocopied for classroom use only

Open All Hours 1

Here are some rules for shop-workers in 1854.

- How long was the store open each day?
- What did employers not like their staff to do?
- Do you think the employers went to church?
- Which activities seem strange to us today?
  - Why did lamps have to be trimmed?
  - Why did pens have to be made?
  - What was 'good literature'?

Today conditions for shop-workers are much better. Do some research and find out what rules shop-workers have today.

- Design and make a Victorian grocer's shop using the foods below and the Open All Hours 2 sheet.

- Which of these products could you find on sale today?

1854

NOTICE

Store must open promptly at 6 a.m. until 9 p.m. all the year round.

Store must be swept, counter, base shelves and showcases dusted.

Lamps trimmed, filled and chimney cleaned, pens made, doors and window opened.

A pail of water and scuttle of coal must be brought in by each clerk before breakfast, if there is time to do so and attend customers who call.

Any employee who is in the habit of smoking Spanish cigars, getting shaved at a barber's shop, going to dances, and other such places of amusement will surely give his employer reason to be suspicious of his integrity and all round honesty.

Each employee must pay not less than one guinea per year to the church, and attend Sunday School every Sunday.

Men are given one evening a week for courting purposes and two if they go to prayer meetings regularly.

After 14 hours work spare time should be devoted to reading good literature.

Open All Hours 2

- Design and make a Victorian grocer's shop using the information from Open All Hours 1.

- List five ways in which shopping for food today is different from this person shopping for food. Give reasons.

What's Cooking?

THE ENGLISHWOMAN'S COOKERY BOOK BY Mrs ISABELLA BEETON. AMPLY ILLUSTRATED

Isabella Beeton wrote many books about cooking and looking after the Victorian household. This is one of her recipes.

Toad-in-the-hole (a Homely but Savoury Dish).

INGREDIENTS:

For the batter:

$1\frac{1}{2}$ lb. of rump steak - 1/-   3 eggs - 3d   4 tblsp of flour - 1d
1 sheep's kidney - 2d   1 pint of milk - 3d $\frac{1}{2}$ spoonful of salt - 1d
pepper and salt to taste - 1d

Cut up the steak and kidney into convenient-sized pieces, and put them into a pie-dish, with a good seasoning of salt and pepper; mix the flour with a small quantity of milk at first, to prevent its being lumpy; add the remainder, and the 3 eggs, which should be well beaten; put in the salt, stir the batter for about 5 minutes, and pour it over the steak. Place it in a tolerably brisk oven immediately, and bake for 1 and a half hours, or rather less. Sufficient for 4 or 5 persons. Seasonable at any time.

Note: The remains of cold beef, rather underdone, may be substituted for the steak, and, when liked, the smallest possible quantity of minced onion or shalot may be added.

Recipe Today
0.5 kilo of sausage, 200 grammes of plain flour, half a litre of milk, 2 eggs, salt and pepper.
Cook the sausages under a grill. Make the batter in a blender. Mix a little flour with some milk, then add more and more so that it is creamy, add the beaten eggs, salt and pepper. Drop the sausages into a dish, pour over the batter and pop into the oven for half an hour or so. Gas mark 7 or 450°F (or use a microwave).

- List the ways Mrs Beeton's recipe is different from the modern one. Give reasons for these differences.
- What aspects of cooking this dish have stayed the same?
- How much does the Victorian meal cost?
- Find out how much the modern recipe would cost.

Mrs Beeton wrote rules for Victorian kitchen staff. Read these, talk about if they were sensible rules for the time and then make up some rules for a modern kitchen.

TO COOKS AND KITCHEN-MAIDS

Cleanliness is the most essential ingredient in the art of cooking; a dirty kitchen being a disgrace both to mistress and maid.
1. *Be clean in your person, paying particular attention to the hands, which should always be clean.*
2. *Do not go about slipshod. Provide yourself with good well-fitting boots. You will find them less fatiguing in a warm kitchen than loose untidy slippers.*
3. *Provide yourself with at least a dozen good-sized serviceable cooking-aprons, made with bibs. These will save your gowns, and keep you neat and clean. Have them made large enough round so as to nearly meet behind.*
4. *When you are in the midst of cooking operations, dress suitably. In the kitchen, for instance, the modern crinoline is absurd, dangerous, out of place and extravagant.*

The Good Seed On The Land

In the early nineteenth century there were few machines to do farm work. Crop yields were low because soils were not always made fertile. A growing population in the towns meant that more and more food was needed.
Farms had to change, but how?
Lord 'Turnip' Townshend had a plan.

"IF YOU PLANT A DIFFERENT CROP IN EACH FIELD OVER 4 YEARS YOU'LL GROW MORE."

"OOH AH, OOH AH!"

COPPICE WOOD

Farmer Giles' farm

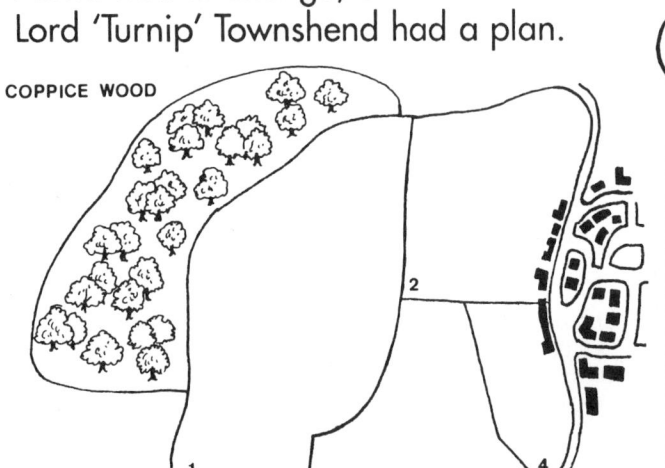

	FIELD 1 10 acres	FIELD 2 8 acres	FIELD 3 5 acres	FIELD 4 2 acres
Year 1	T	C	B	W
Year 2				
Year 3				
Year 4				

'Turnip' Townshend's Advice for farmers

Turnips ~ they will help to clear the ground of weeds, and feed your cows in winter.

Clover ~ puts goodness in your soil, a good fertiliser.

Barley ~
Wheat these are the crops you want but will not get if turnips and clover are not planted.

- Help farmer Giles to work out how to change or 'rotate' the crops in his four fields. Complete the chart. Plant turnips, clover, barley and wheat each year. At the end of four years each field must have had four different crops planted in it.
- Draw on the plan the crops you suggest for year four.
- Barley and wheat were the most important crops. Look where you have planted them in year four. How long will it take to harvest them if it takes ten people a day to harvest one acre?
- Over the years more and more machines were used. What do you think happened to labourers' jobs?

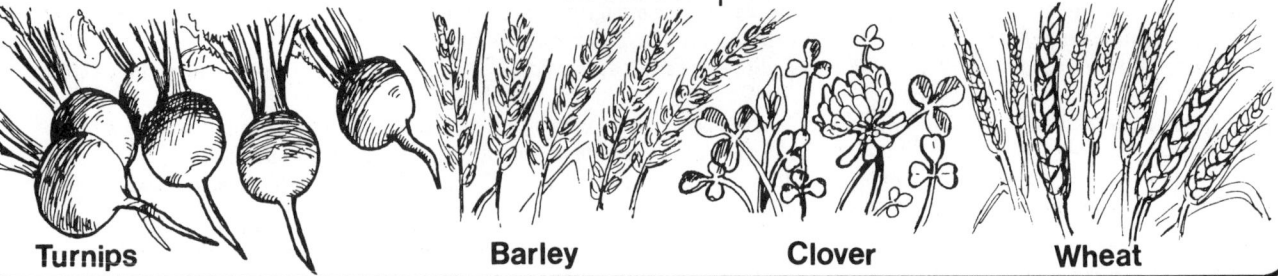

Turnips **Barley** **Clover** **Wheat**

Antiques Roadshow

Imagine that you are an expert on objects from the past, especially Victorian toys. Look at the objects on this sheet.
- What are they? How were they used?
  Use the library to help you find the answers.

"I BOUGHT THIS STRANGE HOUSE AT A CAR BOOT SALE. WHAT IS IT?"

- List a few toys you have that Victorian children would not have had.

Moving Pictures

Victorians were interested in science and technology and used it to amuse themselves. Magic lanterns show us that new photography and electricity were popular towards the end of the 1800s. Before this, children would make 'flick books'. These were easy to make and were an early type of 'movie', in which figures appeared to move.

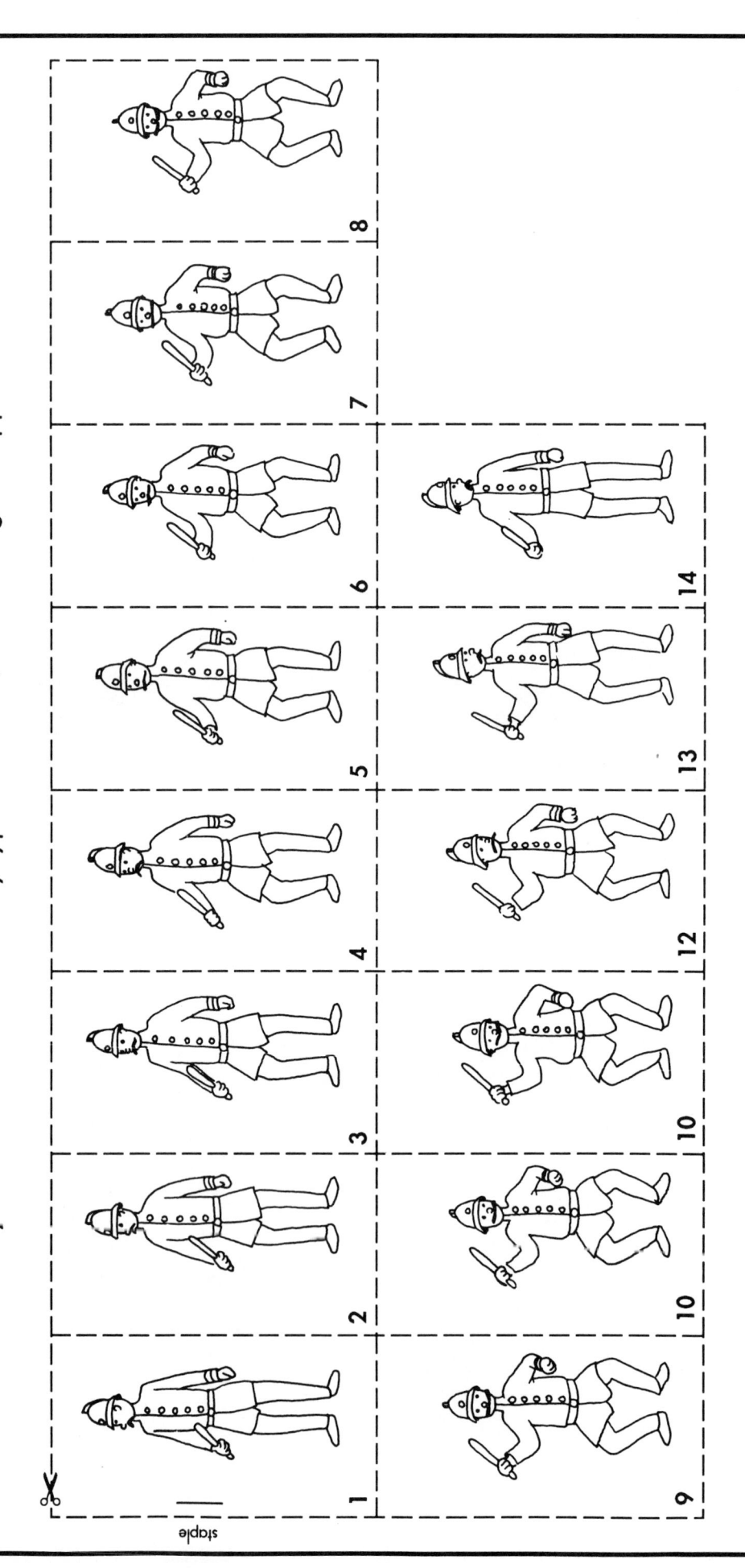

Carefully cut out each picture, stack them with the number 1 on the top. Put a staple through them all. Flick them between your thumb and forefinger to watch your moving picture.

- Make one yourself using a simple figure or object.

Away Day

THE WONDER OF 1851
FROM YORK
TO LONDON AND BACK FOR A CROWN.

THE MIDLAND RAILWAY COMPANY
Will continue to run

TWO TRAINS DAILY
(Excepted Sunday, when only one Train is available)

FOR THE GREAT EXHIBITION,
UNTIL SATURDAY, OCTOBER 11

Without any Advance of Payment

RETURN SPECIAL TRAINS leave the Euston Station on MONDAYS, TUESDAYS, THURSDAYS, & SATURDAYS 11 a.m., on WEDNESDAYS and FRIDAYS at 1 p.m. and EVERY NIGHT (Sundays excepted) at 9 p.m.

First and Second Class Tickets are available for returning any day (except Sunday) up to and including Monday, Oct 20. Third Class Tickets issued before the 6th instant are available for 14 days, and all issued after the 6th are returnable any day up to Monday the 20th.

The Trains leave York at 9-40 a.m. every day except Sunday, and also every day, including Sunday at 7-20 p.m.

Fares to London and Back:—

1st Class 15s.   2nd, 10s.   3rd, 5s.

The Midland is the only Company that runs Trains Daily at these Fares
Ask for Midland Tickets!

Children above 3 and under 12 years of age, Half-price. Luggage allowed—112 lbs. to First Class, 100 lbs. to Second, and to Third Class Passengers.

APPROVED LODGINGS, of all classes, are provided in London for Passengers by Midland Trains. The Agents will give tickets of reference on application, without charge, and an Office is opened in London, at DONALD's WATERLOO DINING ROOMS, 14, Seymour-street, near Euston Station, where an agent is in regular attendance to conduct parties who go up unprepared.

The Managers have much pleasure in stating that the immense numbers who have travelled under their arrangements have been conducted in perfect safety—indeed in the history of the Midland Lines, *no accident, attended with personal injury, has ever happened to an Excursion Train*. In conducting the extraordinary traffic of this Great Occasion the first object is to ensure safety, and that object has hitherto been most happily achieved.

With the fullest confidence, inspired by past success, the Conductors have pleasure in urging those who have not yet visited the exhibition, to avail themselves of the present facilities, and to improve the opportunity which will close on the 11th of October.

All communications respecting the Trains to be addressed to the Managers, for the Company,
John Cuttle & John Calverley, Wakefield;
Thomas Cook, Leicester.

October 2nd, 1851.

T. COOK, PRINTER, 26, GRANBY-STREET, LEICESTER.

Thomas Cook was perhaps the first travel agent. He organised his first excursion in 1841 for a trip to Loughborough from Leicester. His first tour to Switzerland was in 1863 and to America in 1866. His first round the World trip was in 1872.

This poster advertises a 'Thomas Cook' excursion from York to the Great Exhibition.
- In which year was the Great Exhibition?
- How much was a 'crown'?
- What would it cost for a family of two adults and two children aged ten and five to travel first class?
- How many trains from York went to the Exhibition in one week?
- The 'Midland' was one of many different railway companies working in Victorian Britain. Find out the names of some others.
- Design a Victorian poster advertising an excursion from where you live.

Didn't We Have A Lovely Time?

Railways made it possible for more people to travel. Seaside resorts such as Brighton and Blackpool became popular holiday towns. Some towns became very busy and people would crowd on to the beach wearing their everyday clothes, whatever the weather. It was thought wrong for men and women to bathe together so they used different parts of the beach. They changed in special bathing machines which were pulled to the edge of the water by horses.

- Discuss with a friend how a Victorian seaside town is different from one today. Make a large chart like this one to show the differences. The words below will help.

bathing machines yacht
brass band   pier
umbrellas   charabanc
parasols   barrel organ
picnic   hamper

	Victorian Times	Today
Sea		
Beach		
Pier		
Street		

Think About

- Why did people not send holiday postcards to each other until after the 1850s?

- Cut out the picture and make it into a postcard.
- Research how Victorians spent their leisure time and write a postcard to a friend describing your Victorian holiday at the seaside.

That's The Way To Do It!

On the beach there were entertainments to amuse both adults and children. One of the most popular was the Punch and Judy show.

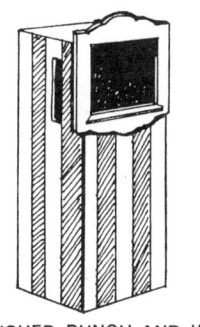

The stage surround

CUT OUT

FINISHED PUNCH AND JUDY

- Use the larger part of a shoe box. Stand it up and cut a hole as in the diagram.
- Colour and cut out the stage surround on this sheet. Cut out the centre and then paste it on the box.
- Cut slits in each side of the box about 1cm x 6cms, level with the opening in the stage surround.
- Cut out the figures, colour them, and staple or stick them on to strips of thick card about 15cms long. Decorate the sides of the box in thick bright stripes.

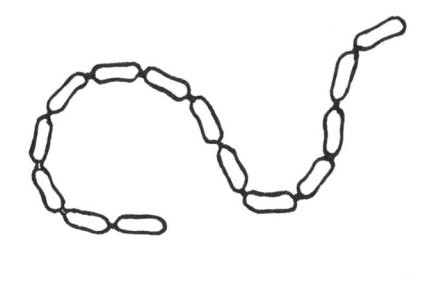

- Invent a story using all the characters. At some point in each story Mr Punch starts a fight!

Shed Street School

Until 1870 there were no laws to make children go to school. Because parents had to pay for their children to attend school, children of poor families often grew up unable to read and write. Schools with classes of sixty or seventy children were common. Some teachers were cruel and often beat their children.

Shed Street School Timetable 1886

9am
9.30am
10.30am
11.30 am
12.30pm Dinner
1.30pm
2.30pm
3.30pm
4.15 Close

- Use the word box to fill in the timetable for Shed Street School.
- How do your lessons, teachers and children compare with those at Shed Street?
- Make a picture timetable to show a day in your school.

WORD BOX

Drill
Arithmetic
Singing
Assembly
Reading
Writing
Scripture

Move With The Times

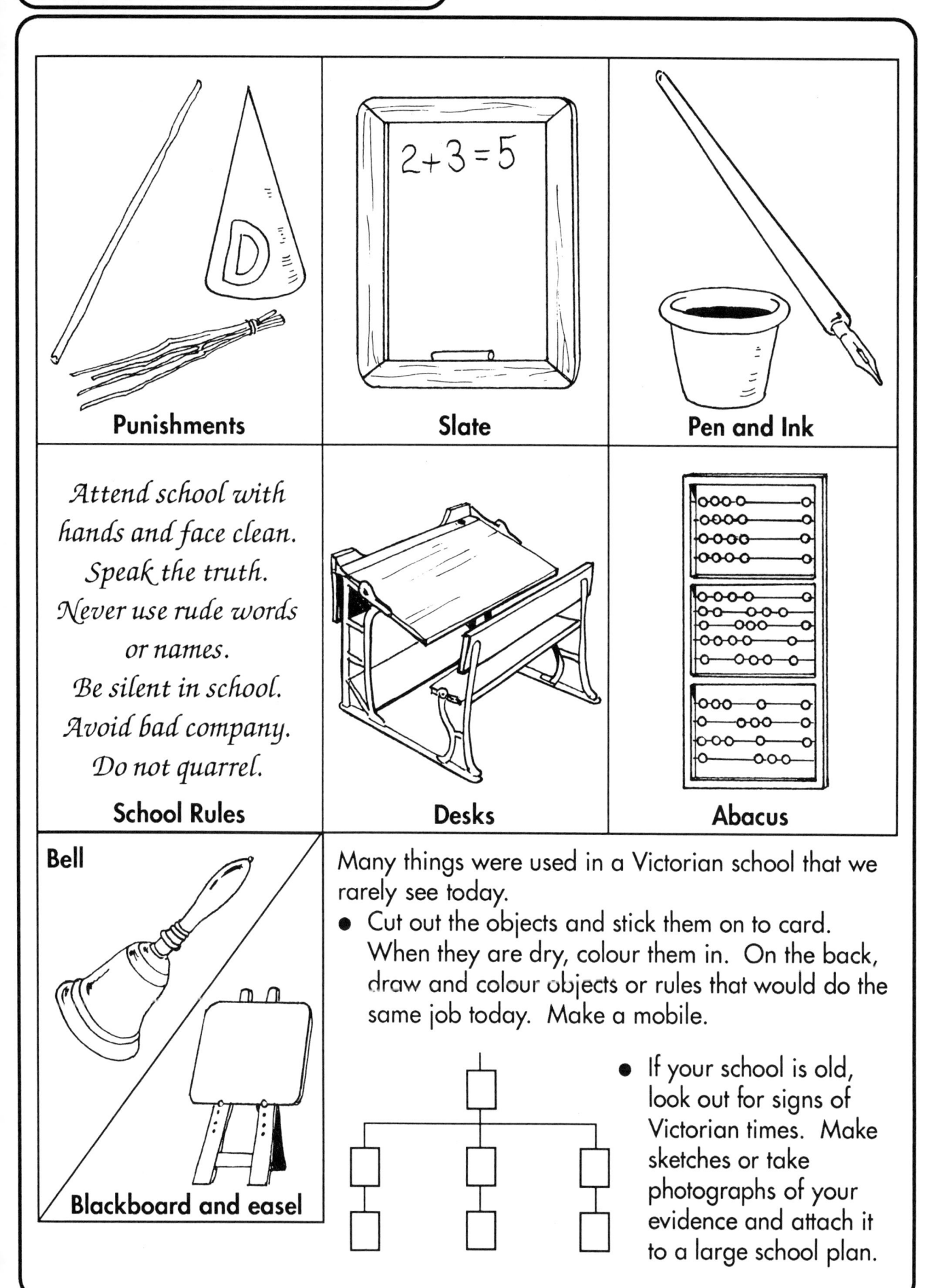

Punishments

Slate

Pen and Ink

Attend school with hands and face clean. Speak the truth. Never use rude words or names. Be silent in school. Avoid bad company. Do not quarrel.

School Rules

Desks

Abacus

Bell

Blackboard and easel

Many things were used in a Victorian school that we rarely see today.

- Cut out the objects and stick them on to card. When they are dry, colour them in. On the back, draw and colour objects or rules that would do the same job today. Make a mobile.

- If your school is old, look out for signs of Victorian times. Make sketches or take photographs of your evidence and attach it to a large school plan.

Folens Ltd. This page may be photocopied for classroom use only

Copy Book

The three Rs reading, 'riting and 'rithmetic were very important in Victorian schools. Every day children practised handwriting. Younger ones tried to form letters on a slate while older ones copied letters and sentences over and over again into a 'copy book'. They used pen and ink and wrote in a style called 'copperplate'. *abcdefghijklmnopqrstuvwxyz*

All the time the teacher would shout instructions, slapping hands if the work was not done well and in silence. Copy these letters and sentences. Use pen and ink if you can. **WORK IN SILENCE!**

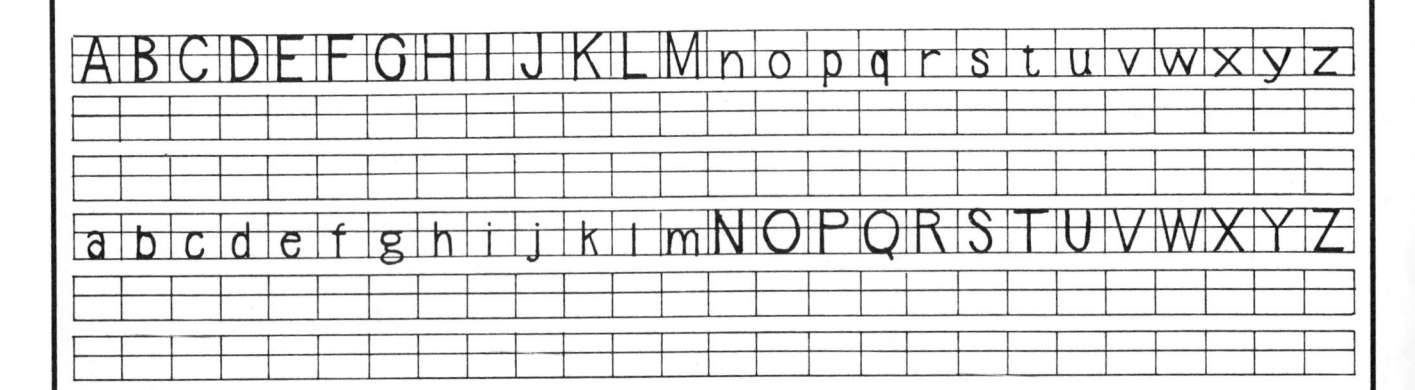

ABCDEFGHIJKLMnopqrstuvwxyz

abcdefghijklmNOPQRSTUVWXYZ

Sixty seconds make a minute. Sixty minutes make an hour.

Twenty four hours a day hath in it. Use each well with all your power.

"Don't make any mistakes boy or it will be the rod for you!"

"There are blots on your page girl. Do this all again now!"

Dear Diary

Mr John Briggs was the headteacher of Prince Ville Board School, Bradford in 1888. Like headteachers today, he had to keep a school log book (a diary), in which school events were recorded.

- Read some of the things that happened in 1888.

> The attendance is very poor. Many children are at home – ill, and about 20 others have gone away into the country.
>
> ---
>
> Edith Ann Arnold (18/V/73) commenced duties as a monitor.
>
> ---
>
> At the reopening on Wednesday morning there were 314 chn present. I have warned Mr Foulds that if his results are not considerably improved I should be obliged to report him to the School Man.t Comm.
>
> ---
>
> Mrs King called to say that her daughter Mary must not be worked in school nor examined, because she has seriously injured her head at the mill. (medical certificate).
>
> ---
>
> July 4th – 8th. The masons have begun to alter the West part of the building. We are now trying to teach ... in a room surrounded by workmen.

- Why were children away during 1888?
- How old was Edith Arnold when she started as a 'monitor' at Prince Ville?
- Why did Mr Briggs have to speak to Mr Foulds?
- Some part-timers worked at a local mill. Do you think the mill was dangerous?
- Why was Prince Ville a noisy place in July?

Your school will have a 'log book'. Have a look at it and copy some unusual entries.

The End Of An Era

Victoria

- Great strides in education. Children had to attend school after 1870.
- Largest Empire. Over a quarter of the world belonged to Britain in 1901.
- More hospitals, doctors and nurses than ever before.
- Victoria Born: 1819 Married: 1840 Died: 1901
- 34 000km of railway lines built. Thousands of bridges, viaducts, tunnels and stations.
- Britain was the workshop of the world.
- Huge increase in time for entertainment and leisure.

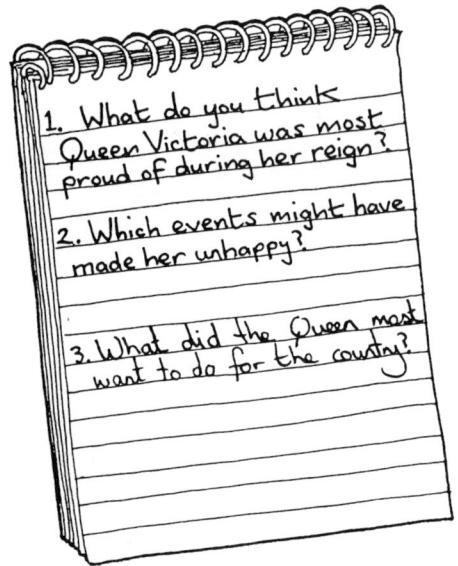

Notebook:
1. What do you think Queen Victoria was most proud of during her reign?
2. Which events might have made her unhappy?
3. What did the Queen most want to do for the country?

Imagine you are a reporter working on the Victorian Times. It is shortly after the Queen's death in 1901.
- Write an article for the newspaper about the life and times of Queen Victoria. Use the headline and the pictures below to help you.
- Write some questions you would want to ask. The notebook will help you.
- Do some research to ask more questions and give answers.

THE VICTORIAN TIMES

Folens Ltd. This page may be photocopied for classroom use only